# Organizing for learning
## in the
## primary classroom

# Organizing for learning in the primary classroom

## A balanced approach to classroom management

JANET R. MOYLES

Open University Press
*Buckingham* • *Philadelphia*

Open University Press
Celtic Court
22 Ballmoor
Buckingham
MK18 1XW

and

1900 Frost Road, Suite 101
Bristol, PA 19007, USA

First Published 1992
Reprinted 1993, 1994 (twice), 1996

Copyright © Janet R. Moyles 1992

A catalogue record of this book is available
from the British Library

*Library of Congress Cataloging-in-Publication Data*

Moyles, Janet R.
    Organizing for learning in the primary classroom : a balanced
approach to classroom management / by Janet R. Moyles.
        p.    cm.
    Includes bibliographical references (p.   ) and index.
    ISBN 0-335-15660-6    ISBN 0-335-15659-2 (pbk.)
    1. Classroom management–Great Britain.  2. Learning.  I. Title.
LB3013.M69   1992
372.11′024′0941–dc20                                      92-5706
                                                            CIP

Typeset by Graphicraft Typesetters Limited, Hong Kong
Printed in Great Britain by St Edmundsbury Press Limited,
Bury St Edmunds, Suffolk

# Contents

# *Acknowledgements*

Written at a time of great change and flux in education, I have constantly felt the need to discuss many aspects of classroom management and organization with colleagues in the University, schools and education in general. To all of these, I express my thanks but particularly to Martin Wenham and Margaret Naylor. Several other teaching colleagues have been kind enough to volunteer a range of advice, photographs and opportunities to visit classrooms, in particular Cherry Fulloway, Steve Winter, Barbara Raper, Jane Kennedy and Lynn Akers.

As usual, my husband Brian has been a tower of strength and a good adviser in relation to classroom plans as well as editing the many drafts of each chapter.

# Introduction:
# Polarizations and balance

Picture the scene: a lively classroom full of motivated and interesting children, some painting canal boats, a group doing science experiments, a few arguing over the solution to a mathematical problem, a group reading in a cosily furnished alcove just off the main area, a cluster of children around the teacher in eager discussion and yet more playing a geography game with another adult. Two other children are moving around the school doing a survey on school dinner preferences and one child is drafting a story on the computer. Everything is calm and orderly and throughout the day children move in and out of various activities, having whole class sessions with the teacher, talking to each other in group and individual situations, working with or alongside the adults in the room, putting materials away, obtaining resources for different activities and interacting in a range of experiences, some of which provide new learning while others provide for the continuous development of existing understanding.

Primary teachers will recognize this scenario and may well think 'So what? Just a normal class on a normal day!' But the underlying systems which have previously been formed are crucial to everything which occurs in that classroom on that day. They go unsung and unnoticed by everyone much of the time, being part of the routines and rituals of primary education. Primary teachers make classroom organization and management look easy – as any student teacher, who has tried to disentangle the strategies used by experienced teachers in maintaining order within the classroom, will tell you! The underlying structure tends to be worthy of comment only when it breaks down for whatever reason and throws our lives into (fleeting) chaos! Witness, for example, when one plimsoll from 30 pairs goes astray: do we ever congratulate ourselves on ensuring that 59 plimsolls are still in their rightful place? It is true to say that the only time we are made fully aware of most organizational and management features is when they go awry or are missing, albeit temporarily.

The complexity of the role of primary teachers and their numerous and diverse responsibilities are unquestionable and go far beyond keeping mere order. In how many other occupations is one person individually and directly responsible for 30 or more other people, for over 6 hours a day, 5 days a week for upwards of 9 months of the year? How many other people, under those conditions, are responsible for almost every aspect of welfare, safety, education, development, for setting working rules and being generally personally and professionally aware of the other people's needs? *In loco parentis* has vast implications.

Ausubel *et al.* (1978: 8) acknowledge the professional skills of the teacher in dealing with the complexities of classroom life:

> . . . in applying a given psychological principle to any particular teaching situation, teachers must exercise considerable professional judgement. They must weigh the claims of one pertinent principle against another; consider relevant aspects of their own preparation and personality, evaluate the momentary situation in the classroom, for example the pupils' state of readiness, motivation, attentiveness, fatigue and current understanding; appraise the adequacy of on-going communication; and take into account differential factors of sex, ability, personality, aspiration and social class membership amongst pupils.

Responding immediately and instinctively to these factors has, according to many researchers, meant that teachers have adopted a reactive style of teaching – a kind of organized and on-going crisis management (see, e.g. Bennett *et al.*, 1984; Galton, 1989). Reactive, rather than proactive, teaching is easily understood in the day-to-day whirl of 'busyness' for both teachers and children. To a certain extent, this is appropriate – if one had to think about every aspect of each movement every time one rode a bike, the potential for falling off would rapidly increase. As McLean (1991: 204) suggests: 'teaching might be described as a never-ending series of on-the-spot decisions, involving an impossibly large number of constantly changing contextual factors and often conflicting concerns'. There is a degree to which being on auto-pilot actually frees the mind to deal with more complex issues, in the way that classroom routines and structures give children a secure base and ensure that they do not have to waste precious 'thinking' time working out the system before they can operate in it (Cullingford, 1991).

At the heart of classroom systems lies the desire to promote children's learning and enthusiasm for learning. As Bull and Solity (1987: 41) emphasize:

> The teacher arranges the classroom environment in ways that enable children to learn more quickly and effectively than they would do alone and [s]he creates a positive classroom atmosphere which promotes enjoyable learning.

In the light of the impact of the many legislated requirements of the National Curriculum and associated assessment procedures, however, teachers have found themselves facing many more organizational and managerial issues and decisions in making provision for learning than ever before (Moyles, 1992). The term 'sweeping the flood with a broom' has taken on new and intense meaning. With one teacher to upwards of 30 children, primary teachers have always felt time, and often space, pressures: now the 'quart-into-a-pint' pot syndrome has to be faced even more strenuously.

The primary classroom is the context in which a wide range of teaching and learning experiences occur, and not just for the children. Because it is familiar, because it has established routines and practices, it is easy to forget how much influence the class base has on all the participants, including 'visitors'. Attempts to implement the many facets of the National Curriculum have shown that the underlying organization and management of the total learning environment is crucial to teachers' and children's feelings of success, achievement and well-being.

Sometimes, however, just because it is taken for granted, teachers have stopped questioning many of the irritating aspects which have become so routine and accepted, yet which nevertheless actually undermine otherwise sound organization and management. Why, for example, do teachers constantly allow interruptions to teaching sessions from those inside and outside the classroom (Varley and Busher, 1989), when it is relatively easy to prevent them if the reasons for their occurrence are determined and remedied? How many times do teachers hear themselves saying the same thing to different groups when efficiency and effectiveness

*The primary classroom is the context in which a wide range of teaching and learning experiences occur.*

would suggest that a whole class statement or discussion would save time and sanity?

Even at this relatively superficial level, there are a number of issues to·be addressed in endeavouring to create time and space for improving and developing curriculum experiences, but a deeper investigation of classrooms provides evidence of other, even more important, factors. In the opening scenario, why were the children organized for learning in that particular way and what were the teacher's intentions? What beliefs did the teacher bring to the organization and management of routines, rules, structures and daily occurrences? What were the prime learning objectives and what influenced the teacher's decision making? At what point were checks made as to the efficacy of the organization for teachers, children and others?

Figure I.1 shows, in diagrammatic form, the many factors implicit within an investigation of primary classroom organization and management and around which some of the basic tenets of this book are built. The school is shown as the mainstay in supporting all the other elements – the classroom and its resources as the focal learning environment, the teachers and teaching, the children and learning. The factors significant to each are also identified and it is these which will form the main basis of the chapters of this book. While there is always a danger in trying

*What beliefs does a teacher bring to the organization and management of routines, rules, structures and daily occurences in the classroom?*

to separate the many strands of such a complex and interwoven system, it is necessary to identify individual elements in order to recreate the whole at some point with greater rigour and understanding. Aspects relating to the whole school and its ethos and other factors external to the classroom, though of acknowledged importance, are mainly implicit within this text for reasons of space and adhering to the main focus.

Throughout the book, the term 'classroom' will be taken to be any area which is the physical base of a class of children, be it an open plan area, the school hall, the mobile in the playground or the alcove at the end of the corridor! 'Organization' is deemed to be that which relates to the context and contents of the classroom setting, including the plans made for teaching and learning: 'management' is related to what teachers do once they have considered their organization in order to ensure both the smooth running of the learning environment *and* fulfilment of intentions (see Fig. I.2). Reorganization will naturally occur and re-occur as part of the evaluation cycle.

This book is aimed primarily at students and new teachers but will inevitably include many aspects which experienced teachers will

*Figure I.1*   A diagram showing the factors implicit within an investigation of primary classroom organization and management

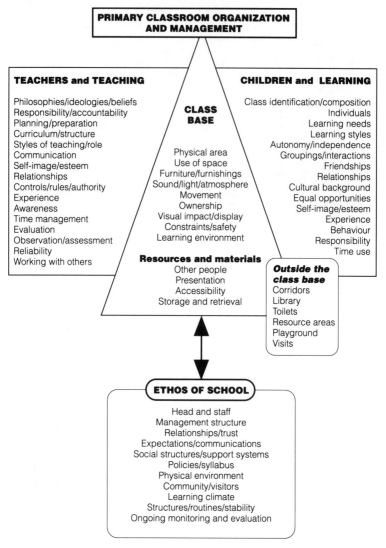

want to revisit. Many adults involved in teaching in the broadest sense throughout the primary school will no doubt also find aspects of interest to their role. Though variations and constraints in classroom organization will exist in relation to both the physical context and the age of the children, quality classroom organization

*Figure I.2*   Organization and management evaluation cycle

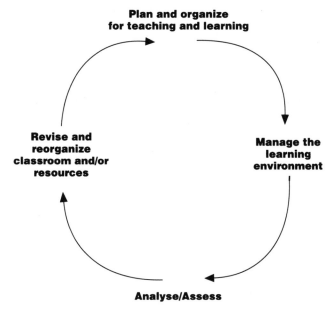

and management is vital irrespective of the age of the children if it is to be an effective learning environment. All classrooms and class bases need to be dynamic, flexible yet committed to order, geared to the systematic and *enjoyable* pursuit of learning, whatever the age group of the children, so much in principle of what is written is applicable across the primary phase. It will be necessary at times, however, for the reader to extrapolate features applicable to their particular age range as it would become turgid and repetitive to keep reiterating differences and similarities across age group needs.

The intention of this book is to explore the complex physical and ideological context in which the many interrelated aspects of teaching and learning occur – *why* do teachers do *what* they do in the classroom context and what does this mean in relation to children and their school learning? Because that which teachers bring to teaching determines the manner in which they undertake their role, opportunities are provided for teachers to reflect on their own values and practices and also to consider innovative and flexible ways forward in coping with new and ever increasing demands on their time and sanity! It is extremely difficult to do justice to the sheer volume of research and theories regarding teaching and learning, though a selective number of research findings are examined and cited in an attempt to integrate crucial or particularly informative aspects of theory with the practical organization and management of the primary classroom. Various aspects of classroom practices at the functional and aesthetic level are explored, many in some detail but, at the end of day, only by delving into the underlying rationales for their beliefs about teaching and learning, will teachers have more than just 'tips' on which to base their present and potential philosophies and context-based outcomes.

It is these philosophies and beliefs which underpin the first chapter. Whatever the physical circumstances of the class base, the teacher's role is paramount and, for this reason, the teacher's perspective is highlighted first. Concentrating on the value systems which structure teachers' classroom intentions and actions and what these mean to children and others, Chapter 1 encourages teachers to consider their own philosophical stance about the role they fulfil and what this means for provision within the physical learning environment. Dilemmas abound, as we shall see, as to the demands of the role, the functions it fulfils and how these, and related issues, are translated into classroom systems.

Chapter 2 investigates the class base as a learning environment, and all which that entails. The physical area, space, furniture, furnishings and other resource and material provision, movement, atmosphere, safety and visual impact, all take their place when considering the creation of a suitable context in which teachers and children spend a sizeable portion of the day. The children themselves are the focus of both Chapters 3 and 4, the former investigating children in the school context, learning styles and beliefs about children as learners and the latter focusing more sharply upon class, group and individualized learning, equal opportunities and behavioural aspects.

Time, or the lack of it, appears to be a key determining factor in the organization and structuring of the teaching and learning environment and the efficient and effective management of time affects both teachers and children alike. School time is potentially limited and needs carefully conceived plans for its use: Chapter 5 addresses the thorny issue of how to maximize achievements within the relatively short 5 or so hours of the school day, and argues that something has to give.

Primary teachers more and more appreciate opportunities for adult assistance in the classroom and making the most profitable and expedient use of such help is included in Chapter 6. The

*Primary teachers more and more appreciate opportunities for adult assistance in the classroom.*

variety of potential sources of classroom assistance are identified and different ways of utilizing these are discussed. The advantages and disadvantages of opening up the classroom to a wide range of people are also considered. Chapter 7 offers suggestions for monitoring and on-going evaluation of all that happens in the classrooms and potentially useful questions for teachers to begin to contemplate further their own practices.

A short concluding chapter then explores briefly issues in relation to the whole school and its ethos, in so far as these affect the teacher's organizational and management decisions in the classroom. It will be shown that the effects are considerably more influential than at first glance appears, not least because of the increasing role played by parents, governors and the community in determining school matters.

At this point, you may be tempted to ask 'Whatever happened to the (National) Curriculum?' The overt and hidden curriculum underlies all classroom planning and, in turn, is influenced by it. At the simplest level, practical science activities, for example, require a certain underlying organization and management structure to be successfully undertaken and these activities then determine what else may or may not simultaneously occur within the class base. The teacher, the children, space, time, resources or the availability of classroom helpers will influence on-going teaching and learning realizations. It is for this reason that the curriculum in general and the National Curriculum in particular have been made an integral part of each chapter. Another rationale for incorporating curriculum in this way is that the more the National Curriculum becomes part of everything we do in an implicit way, the easier effective implementation will become. It emphasizes the pivotal importance and impact which the total curriculum has upon a school, individual classrooms, resources or people.

Issues of behaviour management, so prominent in much writing about classrooms (e.g. Bull and Solity, 1987), have been dealt with similarly through an integrated approach, for it is my contention that most children, given an appropriate learning context that has been created and is managed by a reflective and caring teacher, will readily respond with acceptable behaviour and enjoy their school experience (see also Cullingford, 1991). There are exceptions and these children can only be dealt with individually and with support (see Docking, 1990). Most children want to learn, want to be a part of the unique culture of the primary classroom, and appreciate and respond to a sound working relationship with the teacher.

The paramount importance of sound organization and management of learning has never before demanded greater prominence: the time available in school is still finite, the curriculum and other demands are seemingly infinite. Resolving this dilemma is not easy and some 'short-term pain for long-term gain' is likely, for it requires teachers to delve into their own philosophies, examine their own values, decide on new priorities and have the courage and conviction to put these into practice. In a way, it is very personal yet far more enlightening when shared. In the first chapter, we will start out together on this process.

# 1

---

## Teachers and teaching: Beliefs and values

As a new teacher, anxious to know where to start with my first class, I remember being told emphatically by a headteacher to 'Start with the children – the rest will take care of itself.' The obvious child-centredness underlying this belief appealed very much to me as a protagonist for the 'whole child' approach. It is easy to imagine my distress when I quickly discovered the inaccuracy of this advice. It did not take me too long to realize that if I was not prepared to receive the children when they arrived each day, so much time was spent by all of us rushing around after materials, sharpening pencils, finding resources and so on, that there was little time to make vital relationships with individuals.

The next phase in my learning, therefore, thrust me in quite the opposite direction, an understandable (but now unforgivable) response! 'Start with the organisation and then there will be *time* for the children' became my self-targeted advice. This was equally, of course, potentially inaccurate and naive. Organization *is* a means to an end and not an end in itself but, nevertheless, classroom organization and management at all levels has other underlying factors determining both its needs and its implementation. As Alexander *et al.* (1989: 299) suggest: 'notwithstanding the undoubted importance of classroom layout and organization, they are but the framework within which the acts and interactions central to teaching and learning take place'.

In a recent survey conducted among primary teachers, I asked what was their first consideration in planning classroom organization at the beginning of the school year: significantly, the answer 'children' was given by 100 per cent of the respondents. It seems likely that this is, in fact, a contradiction between philosophy and practice. It is actually unrealistic at the beginning of a school year to start by thinking about an unknown class of children and it is far more likely that the pressing needs of the physical environment will be paramount. But it is over this physical environment that teachers will bring their knowledge, skills and values to bear in order to create, in their view, an appropriate environment for learning. This highlights exactly the focus of this chapter, which attempts to examine, through practical examples wherever possible, how teaching is driven by a kind of rhetoric which is frequently at odds with reality. Examination of a selection of the various factors and some of the wealth of literature should help to establish a foundation of strengths from which teachers can explore practice.

## Philosophies, ideologies, beliefs and values

What teachers believe and value, both professionally and personally, underpins everything they do and the way they do it (see, e.g. Claxton, 1989; Cullingford, 1989; Nias, 1989). It is therefore a truism to say that teachers must identify what it is they *do* believe about teaching and learning and their role in it if they are to have a foundation for contemplating other classroom factors. Consider your own responses to the following statements made by teachers. Do you agree with their views? Why or why not?

---

ACTIVITY 1

1  I think I'm fairly traditional in the classroom: children need to learn the basic skills, don't they?
2  We do things quite informally here: the children have a lot of choice and are really independent.
3  It's important that the children learn things for themselves: so much better than being told, isn't it?
4  Children don't learn by osmosis, do they? They need to be taught.
5  The children are grouped by ability because it's important that the children of lower ability don't hold back the brighter ones.
6  I think children should sit with their friends. After all, school is a social setting too.

7 It's important that they get through the work in the morning and then we can do more arty things in the afternoon.
8 I work an integrated day: children just don't see things as separate subjects, do they?

---

Whatever your responses, how the underlying beliefs and values which surface are established is a complex mixture of training, experiences, cultural circumstances, personality and even political expectations. In recent years, the media has played a prominent role in establishing and sponsoring many national beliefs and values about education, schooling and the role of the teacher.

A number of models in relation to teaching styles and teachers' roles have been presented through classroom investigations and theoretical treatises (see Dadds and Lofthouse, 1990). Teachers have tried valiantly to respond to suggestions of 'good practice' but these, coupled with the concurrent demands of curriculum, parents, governors, the community, colleagues, accountability systems and children's needs, have actually left teachers in a seemingly never-ending whirl of action and reaction which is exhausting at best and demoralizing at worst. There is confusion at every level as to what is appropriate pedagogical practice and teachers, in many cases, actually welcomed the National Curriculum for providing a framework for at least the 'what' of teaching (Thomas, 1991). But even this is undergoing such revisions (welcome though they may be) that, again, the ground is moving and uncertainty prevails.

Such 'dilemmas of teaching' are well documented (see, e.g. Berlak and Berlak, 1981; Galton, 1989) and could be said to stem from the fact that there are so few prescriptions in education – something is right for someone some of the time! The difficulty is getting the classroom formula 'right' most of the time. Clearly, at the heart of what teachers do is a belief in the impossible! Teaching nine subjects, a host of other curriculum areas, taking responsibility for social and moral learning, being a friend, mentor, substitute parent and care-giver requires teachers to assume almost superhuman characteristics. It is no wonder that we clutch at the familiar and groan at the welter of seemingly new innovations.

A return to some first principles of pedagogy is necessary (Simon, 1981). From the wealth of literature, but more importantly from discussions with teachers (some of whose comments are given above), it is possible to ascertain a few areas which create the most dilemmas for teachers and which have a major influence over decisions about organizing and managing the classroom. Although extremely complex in substance, these are mostly related to acquired beliefs about:

- child-centredness and individualized learning;
- teaching intentions and constraints;
- styles of teaching and learning;
- children's perceived ability, or lack of ability; and
- managing finite time.

These, in turn, have often been formed from polarized views (Alexander, 1984; Cortazzi, 1991) handed down to us as educational 'traditions', e.g. child-centredness ↔ teacher domination, formal ↔ informal methods, experiential/discovery learning ↔ exposition, and progressivist ↔ traditionalist beliefs. We can readily see a hint of many of these popular polarized views expressed in the comments of teachers recorded earlier.

While not unhelpful in themselves in defining something of the parameters of potential thinking and practice, such polarizations are 'dangerous' in that they may lead teachers to believe they *ought* to be adopting one method or the other even when this is clearly not the case (Riseborough, 1985). Continuous 'discovery' learning of the first-hand, practical experience kind, for example, could well lead to children having to reinvent the wheel with every activity. While necessary in some circumstances, such as exploring materials, properties and textures, it is actually inefficient as a learning strategy in other situations, for example having to discover every mathematical principle or art technique. It is possible, of course, still to 'discover' through being told something, but this can easily be forgotten if polarized extremes dominate thinking. Similarly, learning situations that are all exposition are equally inefficient for the learner in that any one of us can only absorb a certain amount at any one time (Halford, 1980).

On the positive side – and of greater importance – polarizations permit a broad view of the 'middle ground' which is both realistic and a more propitious philosophical stance for primary teachers given the diversity of both the children's needs and the broad curriculum demands. Figure 1.1 indicates how this situation should offer teachers a sense of equilibrium in relation to classroom organization and management, with a requisite *balance* between teacher and learner needs. Figures 1.2 and 1.3 show the converse of this arrangement, where the domination of either group will create a sense of imbalance and potential instability.

*Figure 1.1*   A balanced approach to primary classroom organization – a sense of equilibrium

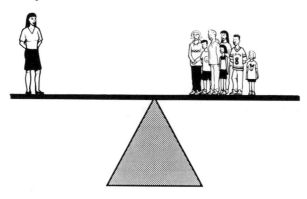

*Figure 1.2*   Imbalance – the teacher dominates

Contemplation of how far one's own teaching situation reflects these models is worthwhile. For now, it is necessary to investigate each of the principles identified above, its relationship to the classroom and the interrelatedness of different aspects. Discussion on the crucial issue of time management, however, will be left until Chapter 5.

### Child-centredness and individualized learning

By being 'child-centred', primary teachers normally mean that they are concerned with the development and learning of individual

*Figure 1.3*    Imbalance – the children dominate!

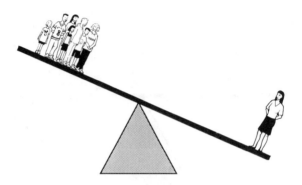

children and that identified individual needs take priority in teaching, a view which has stemmed from the principles of the Plowden Report (1967). This approach, however, also means starting from a standpoint of individual *differences* (Stones, 1979) which, in turn, means a differentiated curriculum as a basic requirement. In practice, while the former may be a sound principle, the latter is virtually impossible to achieve, as many studies have shown (e.g. Bennett *et al.*, 1984; Alexander *et al.*, 1989) given the present teacher/child ratios. Reducing class sizes, however, would not change the fact that children actually have more *similarities* in terms of learning potential than they have differences.

The manifestation of a child-centred philosophy in the classroom has been classes of busy individuals, for whom teachers have provided a variety of tasks but who have received only cursory attention, much of that being managerial and related to keeping children on-task rather than engaged with learning (see, e.g. King, 1978; Bennett *et al.*, 1984; Bennett and Kell, 1989). This is highly obvious if one does a basic calculation of usable hours in the school day. With assemblies, playtimes, lining up, settling down and moving around the school, at best there is likely to be between 3½ and 4 hours a day teaching and learning time. Divide this by the number of children and in most primary classes contact time with individuals amounts to a very few minutes each day or week (4 hours × 60 minutes = 240 ÷ 32 children = 7.5 minutes a day each child × 5 days = 37.5 minutes per week). Theoretical time is, however, very different from the reality, as West and Wheldall (1989) showed in relation to infant children having to wait for teacher attention.

If one starts from the standpoint, as arguably the National Curriculum has attempted to do, of determining teaching needs according to common experiences relevant to particular ages, then the teacher's role becomes one of 'deliberate development of such skills and abilities in all their children' (Simon, 1981: 139). This need not necessarily mean that individual needs are not recognized and addressed but rather that children who require a specific programme will be the minority rather than the majority, making planning for learning far more realistic. Neither does this mean advocating a return to whole class teaching as the norm: rather, whole class *thinking* in terms of planning modified by individual considerations as necessary. There is implicitly a general responsibility for individual schools and staffs to modify the overall curriculum according to their perceptions of appropriateness for their particular pupils. *Primary Practice* (Schools Council, 1983) is probably the only document to really attempt to integrate a view of child-centredness with subject curriculum planning and is worth revisiting.

Individualization highlights one of the dilemmas previously discussed: teachers feel under stress in attempting to meet all individual needs because this is what they traditionally believe they should be doing. Balanced against this is something of a guilt feeling because the one-to-many classroom reality means that they attempt to group, perhaps by reading level or maths level, but then the activities are still approached mostly individually through, for example, scheme workbooks (Tizard, *et al.*, 1988). But, as has already been identified, this could be readily revised if teachers review their overt practice for dealing with the concept of individuality.

An over-emphasis on the individual also potentially denies the social dimension of schooling and a most important aspect of learning which is highlighted in 'interactionist'/'constructivist' theories of learning (e.g. Pollard, 1985; Bruner, 1986). Children construct meaning and thereby learn through interactions with others – both adults and children. If a classroom is organized and managed on a highly individualistic perspective, it is unlikely that teachers will plan and prepare the classroom with a view to creating specific opportunities for learning through interactions such as peer tutoring or collaborative group learning (discussed in Chapter 4).

Once the principle of individual similarities, and thereby enhanced collaboration, is recognized, further opportunities become evident. Primary teachers have rightly emphasized social learning (Ashton, 1981), yet observed practice has shown that social groupings amount to little more than seating arrangements and that cooperative and collaborative group work rarely occurs (Galton *et al.*, 1980). Once teachers are 'freed' of the constraints of extreme individualized perspectives and a balanced view generated, all those aspects of teaching and learning which require an essentially social element – for example, discussion on issues of concern such as anti-racist education, or children's autonomy (Rowlands, 1987) – become possibilities from any number of angles, with or without the teacher taking a prominent role.

There is always a danger, too, in classrooms in which a highly individualistic perspective predominates, that child-centredness may become child-domination: this is not so outrageous as at first appears. Consider the teacher who says 'I like the children to decide what to focus on each day. It's no good flogging something which they aren't really interested in.' It is quite possible for this philosophy to be interpreted as the children 'doing their own thing' all day which may well lead to learning but may also be impossible to relate to the curriculum-for-all stance suggested earlier. The child is, therefore, dominating the curriculum and, for the teacher, meeting its many demands for every child then becomes near impossible. It will also be argued in the next section, that a main role of the teacher is in developing a form of negotiated learning with the children so that teaching intentions can be met within a balanced framework of the children's interests and needs. Instead of emphasizing individual differences within teaching plans, we need to heed the advice of Powell and Solity (1990: 60), who emphasize 'the benefits of deriving general principles of teaching, which can help all children experience success at school'.

Taking this concept of the child as essentially unique but necessarily one part of a whole in terms of classroom and curriculum needs, how we decide on intentions for teaching and then deal with the constraints in practice is the next focus.

## Teaching intentions and constraints

Planning for learning is about setting aims and objectives, converting them into teaching intentions and then allowing the children, through various activities, to translate them into a whole spectrum of knowledge, skills and understandings appropriate to them. The formal curriculum can only be one part of the child's overall learning: there is also the influence of the ubiquitous 'hidden'

*The child is essentially unique but still one part of a whole in terms of classroom and curriculum needs.*

curriculum (Hartley, 1987) and learning, both positive and negative, from the peer group culture (Pollard, 1987). Intentions for teaching need constantly to be balanced, as we have seen, between thinking of holistic teaching needs and individual learning needs.

This aside, most primary teachers have a very clear view of the whole curriculum, including the National Curriculum, and take great care over planning for its implementation. Whether topic or subject orientated, class, group or individual methods, to accommodate what is felt desirable requires specific classroom organization and management. Take a moment to consider what you would do in the following situation:

---

ACTIVITY 2

It is your intention after morning break today to introduce a new science topic on forces and energy through a class demonstration using some simple toys. You have organized all the necessary resources, you know it will be interesting and motivating to the children and your plans have been carefully conceived. The rest of the morning for your Year 3 class will be reinforcement work on forces and energy in specific groupings to maximize learning, and you have identified a particular activity for two children who take more time than the others to absorb new concepts.

At the beginning of the day, however, a child arrives with some ladybirds in a jar which she shows to the rest of the class during registration. In the first half of the morning, it is clear that these ladybirds have become the focus of much interest.

- What do you do about your after-play science session plans?
- Why?

Whatever your response, the issue highlights yet another di-lemma for teachers: the balance between pursuing their intentions for children's learning or allowing the children's interests to deter-mine what happens. If teachers are diverted from their original intentions in the short term, albeit in the interests of children's motivation, it is unlikely that they will even begin to meet neces-sary curriculum objectives in the long term. The natural ability of young children to be 'extremely good at learning' (Holt, 1991: 160) and divergent in their approach (Fisher, 1990) means that, to a certain extent, they will learn from whatever is provided. Rogers (1983: 27) believes that teachers should use sufficiently perceived structure so that students can comfortably start to work. It is worth remembering, too, that Makins (1969: 196) found evidence, when interviewing 1200 primary children, that *what* they do matters less to children than *how* they are taught. Other research (Ellsworth and Monahan, 1989: 72) suggests that children generally show more cooperation and support for teachers who display expertise and consistency of expectations in the teaching role, which has to be linked to teaching from a baseline of clear objectives.

In formulating the objectives for a particular activity or session, teachers will also have developed insights into what learning can be anticipated and how this may be assessed. Once this framework has been abandoned, so has the structure and much of the potential for developing the next stage of learning based on assessment of present understandings. 'The road to hell is paved with good inten-tions' – or so it must seem at times to the hard-working primary teacher!

Calderhead (1984: 22) suggests that: 'Effective classroom management can be viewed as essentially concerning the achievement and maintenance of pupils' involvement in teacher-prescribed or teacher approved activities.' Getting children then to take ownership over their activities lies in the skill of the teacher. Bennett *et al.* (1984: 219) supported this in their research in top infant classrooms:

> ... the essence of any good management strategy is to provide a system of rules and procedures which will optimize the main purpose of the work setting. In classrooms therefore management should provide the framework for the teachers' learning intentions.

The caring relationship which primary teachers build with their classes means that this 'loss' of intentions apparently has no major effect on the children – or does it? Certain effects are possible to discern (and some of the studies already cited bear witness to this), for example, children who constantly need reassurance and guidance as to what to do next, the 'I need to sharpen my pencil' or the 'rubbers' brigade (yes, I have had them in my class too!). It is very easy to feel 'alone in a crowd' in the primary classroom – for children and teacher alike.

A balanced resolution seems both simple and complex. If the classroom is to be a happy and productive place, children need a stable but exciting environment in which learning is almost irresistible, a place in which the process of learning is so stimulating that they are required to use and acquire certain skills and understandings in order to participate fully in what is on offer! They also need to establish ownership over their own learning (Moyles, 1991), but this does not mean that it cannot be teacher-inspired in the first place.

By writing down or keeping firmly to the front of their minds the intentions set, teachers can still be flexible in allowing children to determine the means by which they achieve the required outcomes. This, in turn, requires teachers to *share learning intentions with children*. Children questioned about a teacher's intentions have more often than not reported little to classroom enquirers about actual learning. Calderhead (1984: 61) feels that 'pupils can often regard the object of activities as coming up with right answers as opposed to learning and, in some cases, this concern predominates their thinking'. Cullingford (1991: 18) suggests that children are often presented with 'activities rather than explanations', and

Bennett *et al.* (1984: 213) found that classroom tasks 'had in common a teacher stress on procedural rather than cognitive aims'. In a fascinating comparative study between French and English primary teachers (Broadfoot *et al.*, 1988), significant cultural differences were found between the teachers. French teachers saw children as 'students' and were more concerned with approaches to teaching and the content of the curriculum. English teachers, in contrast, emphasized the 'whole child' and were more concerned with classroom activities and relationships. The differences, although subtle, were significant, though each system clearly has its strengths and undoubtedly each could learn something from the other about the broadest concept of being a teacher.

Much of what has been said almost requires a reappraisal of the term 'teacher'. Many alternatives have been offered over the past few years – facilitator, enabler, instructor, initiator and, of course, organizer. While the role of teacher is important in all these ways, the role of the learner is crucial. Children have an innate ability to learn (Rogers, 1983; Holt, 1991). The interactionist/constructivist approaches emphasize the close relationship between the roles of teacher and learner. Teachers help children to learn not just about the curriculum, but how to be a learner (Nisbet and Shucksmith, 1986: 28), how to accept responsibility for one's own learning and to understand metacognitive processes ('thinking about thinking'; see Turner, 1984: 12), as well as learning themselves (Wenham, 1991).

## Too many, too few, too little

The perceived constraints on organizing and managing for learning in this way are usually related to a large number of children, lack of space in the classroom, lack of appropriate resources or sufficient quantity of resources, lack of support systems, peer and parental pressures upon teachers and schools, and insufficient time, all of which will be covered in later chapters of the book. Suffice it to say for the present, that many teachers overcome enormous numbers of difficulties by thinking flexibly and by involving the children in making classroom decisions about storage or materials or how to work in a given way. Even having large numbers of children can be turned to advantage by the thoughtful teacher. Children are a major resource in themselves, as many teachers have discovered. Inexperienced in some ways they may be, but the culture of school is as much theirs as it is the teachers. Many are very intuitive and most enjoy the challenge of organizing something for themselves, even the youngest. Consider the following example and how far you feel the teacher had all the necessary opportunities for following her learning intentions and utilizing the children's skills.

---

## ACTIVITY 3

The teacher wanted to involve a class of 6-year-olds in planning a day visit to a local canal lock. Her overall objective was for the children to experience (1) an operational lock and (2) a canal tunnel via a boat trip. In addition, it was to be an enjoyable day out as a culmination to some of the work they had been doing on waterways. But by also planning for children's involvement in the preparation for the visit, they would gain a sense of ownership over the visit and the learning experiences and begin to gain new insights and understanding of their own capabilities. She structured where they would begin by suggesting that, during the morning, one group of children collected a list from all the others of what they thought needed organizing for a successful day visit. Later in the morning, this list was shared with the whole class and showed surprising sensitivity on the part of the children to their own and others' needs, the list including all the obvious things like booking the coach and the boat, but also including things like the need for there to be toilets, a dry place if it was wet to eat lunch, seats for the teachers and parent helpers and somewhere for the children to have a 'playtime'. The necessary jobs were then identified and allocated to groups of children, who wrote letters to parents, made necessary enquiries of the canal authorities and bookings (with the help of the school secretary), even deciding on what it was sensible to take for lunch, e.g. chocolate was out as it would melt on a hot day (which they had decided it would be by watching the weather forecasts at home!). Needless to say, the day was a great success and during the end-of-year discussions with the teacher, the event had clearly been a highlight of the children's experiences.

---

This teacher showed an objective approach to teaching and meeting learning intentions while still allowing the children to be responsible for their own learning. As we shall now see, this may well be related to her own learning style.

## Styles of teaching and learning

Why are you reading this book? Do you feel that you learn from this kind of written exposition? Or do you learn better by going back into the classroom and actually doing some of the things for yourself? Perhaps you like to share your learning experiences with someone else or maybe you like someone else to show you how to begin undertaking something you want to achieve? Perhaps you are on the verge of a new discovery and all you need is someone to give you the last link to make it all clear?

These are genuine questions about our own styles of learning, ones which we rarely, if ever, stop to ask ourselves. Yet a very basic and insistent message, extracted from a growing amount of literature, is that we tend to teach in the style by which we essentially like to learn (see Mahlios, 1989: 97). Entwhistle (1988: 231) says of the link between this concept and that of polarized views:

> Each opposed view of education is, in part, an expression of the theorist's own preferred way of thinking. He may be describing little more than which type of learning he himself would find most beneficial. . . . Somehow the approach to teaching must take account of the variety of styles of learning among the learners, not just the preference of the teacher.

So a first requirement in achieving the necessary balance must be to identify ourselves as learners and, in so doing, begin to understand the often subconscious motives behind our own teaching styles and methods.

Various theories regarding teaching styles in general have been proffered (see Wittrock, 1986), but in relation to *adult learning* Mumford (1982: 61) suggests four different modes which he relates as:

1 *Activitists*: those who enjoy the here and now, are dominated by immediate experiences, thrive on challenge but get bored with implementation and long-term consolidation and who do not necessarily recognize problems.
2 *Reflectors*: those who stand back and ponder, collect data and analyse it, consider all possible angles, and are cautious.
3 *Theorists*: those who are keen on basic assumptions, theories, principles, models; are rational and logical, detached and analytical; are able to assemble disparate facts into coherent theories. Like to make things tidy and fit.
4 *Pragmatists*: those who search out new ideas, experiment, brim

with lateral thinking, and see 'problems' as new opportunities and 'challenges'.

It is likely that elements of all these are present in all teachers but that one main mode surfaces more clearly than others. These also suggest a relationship with personality traits and character- istics (Anderson and Burns, 1989). How many teachers recognize themselves within these frameworks? Is there evidence in the class- room of a relationship between the teacher's preferred styles of learning and the way learning is presented to the children? In terms of organizing for learning, this may well have some very direct consequences, with the various headings conjuring up inter- esting generalizations. Activists are likely to have very busy class- rooms, with a wide variety of on-going activities, the teacher being involved in everything and it could all look rather chaotic. They are perhaps most likely to agree with a highly child-centred ap- proach, whereas reflectors may present activities very carefully in a step-by-step fashion and, while having concern for individuals, would analyse group and class needs and offer a very calm ethos. Theorists are likely to be teachers whose classrooms are very neatly organized with a place for everything, but who may get quite upset by anything which they deem to be illogical. Pragmatists seem to offer a technological approach and it is likely that the class would be deeply involved in problem-solving activities and that the management of learning may be swamped in a wealth of on-going ideas.

The more serious side is that teachers face yet more dilemmas in this area on two counts: first, adults' fundamental learning style is often subsumed in the kind of learning which was imposed upon them in school and, secondly, whatever the rhetoric, the school system in general still appears to respond better to the needs of reflectors and theorists by its very traditions than it does to those of activists and pragmatists. So even though teachers may actually have learning styles nearer to the latter, conformity from the system and colleagues (Nias, 1989) requires them to adopt the former.

For this reason, a 'formal' teaching style is one of the easiest to understand and absorb and, therefore, likely to be resorted to at any time of uncertainty. Teachers' own backgrounds of relative success in education (a majority have completed 3 or more years of higher education, most now to degree level) and their motivation to succeed, means that their own values are manifested through the type of teaching they received which put them where they are now. Most 'academic' learning is deemed to take place at secondary school (see Cullingford, 1991) and perhaps college or university, much of it of the formal exposition type. Quantity factors, such as getting through as much as possible of a syllabus, tend to lead to exposition. Teachers mostly remember this aspect as leading to their 'success' and, therefore, deeply embedded in their subconscious is the belief that this method will also ensure success for children even though later training may have suggested a very different kind of more balanced approach. (The same is equally true, though often for different reasons, of parental pressure for 'real' work-related activities.) This belief is in stark contrast to, and contradicts even more, the equally deep-seated notions of child-centredness and basing teaching on the corporate and individual needs of children already discussed. So many classrooms show an uneasy attempt to reconcile a subconscious desire for exposition with experiential learning known to have distinct benefits for primary age children. As an example, children are seated in groups (often with their backs to where the teacher is able to speak to them all) so that they can share experiences with various materials and activities but then there is much shuffling, loss of concentration and time wasting when the teacher wishes to teach the whole class directly. The type of class seating arrangement shown in Fig. 1.4 exemplifies this point.

Exposition is, in teaching terms, quicker to execute, but is more wasteful in terms of acquired understandings (Claxton, 1984), whereas first-hand experiences focus more on the learners' needs and offer opportunities for those children whose essential learning style is potentially that of an activist or pragmatist (discussed further in Chapter 3). What this also highlights is two other main points in this section:

1 The teacher must also constantly be a learner in the classroom (Claxton, 1990).
2 There is potentially a conflict between teacher as teacher and teacher as person (Woods, 1990: 181).

Proactive, reflective teaching (Pollard and Tann, 1987), as discussed in the Introduction, requires teachers who will learn from what happens in the classroom not just about the children but about their role in teaching and learning processes. This, in turn, requires that teachers periodically stand back and become observers of the learning environment. How is the space in the classroom used? How do children move about? Who learns particularly well by interacting with whom? This kind of opportunity for reflection

*Figure 1.4* Group seating arrangement, but can they all see the teacher?

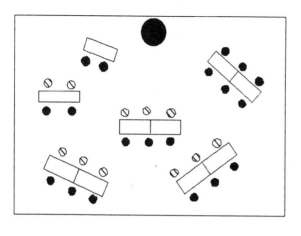

Key:  ● = children who will be able to see teacher

○ = children who will not be able to see teacher readily

● = teacher

can only occur in classrooms where the teaching style adopted requires independence and personal responsibility on the part of the children, who should not then need the teacher to support every aspect of their learning. Children who are clear about the purpose of the activities, have the necessary materials to hand and are trained to acquire them for themselves and who use other children as a resource for information and guidance, are unlikely to need the constant support of the teacher. Teachers usually suggest that this is what *they* want of children, but then get drawn into acting in a way which results in children becoming dependent. A classic situation is seen regularly in classrooms. It goes something like this:

> *Teacher*: I am going to work with this group for the next ten minutes. The rest of you know what you are doing and can get on. Are there any queries before we start? No? Right! (Goes to sit with group readers and indicates that they should begin)
>
> *Child from another group*: (walking over and standing by the teacher's shoulder) I can't do this page.

*Teacher*: I told you not to interrupt me. Go and sit down.
*Child*: But Mr S. – I really can't do it – it's hard!
*Teacher*: Well I suppose as you have already interrupted me
... look it's just like the sums you did earlier (turns back
child's book two pages). See. Nadine could help you. Go
and see her.

The teacher's style, apparently appropriate, resulted in an outcome which was not as anticipated – why? The children were told
clearly of the teacher's intentions but, unfortunately, they were
not then told why it was important not to interrupt or what they
could do (consult other children, look back in their workbooks,
and so on) if they had a query. In the moment of responding to
this child's expressed needs – which may or may not have been
genuine – the work of other children was interrupted and the
teacher was seen to act inconsistently, thereby confirming for
another occasion that, whatever he may say, children will get a
response if they seek one. If this is a child who constantly inter-
rupts, it could be that the level of work is inappropriate to meet
the child's needs rather than a behaviour difficulty. Calderhead
(1984: 21) is clear:

> ... effective classroom managers ... spend more time than
> their less effective colleagues communicating to pupils their
> expectations for classroom behaviour, explaining the proce-
> dures by which the work of the class is to be carried out and
> the reasons for such procedures.

Telling *that* you are doing something, (e.g. 'working with this
group'), does not explain *why* or what your expectations of the
others will be.

The teacher's knowledge of the children is also vital, but it must
not be forgotten that the children get to know teachers and their
styles *and* they well know how to manipulate them (just as they
know how to manipulate parents). Both teachers and learners are
constantly data gathering!

This does not mean being a dragon all the time! Children appreciate teachers being human – witness their faces when they see
you actually shopping in the local supermarket! Being friendly but
keeping a distance is a trait valued in teachers by children and,
above all else, primary children like teachers who are consistent
and fair. There is also something of the thespian in every teacher.
However one feels, the classroom 'show' must go on. This is not
to say that teachers are denying themselves; rather, they need to

be somewhat 'larger than life' in attempting to carry out the many characters implicit in the teacher role. Feigned shock or distress, surprise and delight and their outward manifestation (whatever the inward reality), all come readily to teachers and are, without a doubt, skills acquired with being 'on stage' all day, a factor which decidedly adds to the stress of the role, for how many actors and actresses are required to be on stage for up to 6 hours a day, 5 days a week?

Teachers understandably wish to support children, but is the best way to support someone making them reliant upon you? This kind of consistency and balance of teaching style, far from taking away the children's ownership of learning, actually places the onus on children to be responsible, sensitive to others and independent in the classroom. These are surely virtues we wish to inculcate. Whether teachers feel every child is able to adopt this learning style will depend on how they view the children's potential.

Teachers also value and thrive on this sense of ownership and responsibility, which is easily proven given the context in the early days of the National Curriculum when professionalism was seen to be under attack and morale took a tumble from which it is still recovering. More specifically, however, because teachers are so involved in their role, onslaughts to professional values also become threatening at a personal level and it is difficult for teachers, because of their highly social and involved view of their own role, to extricate the person from the role they fulfil. In working some time ago with teachers on aspects of teacher appraisal and self-evaluation (Moyles, 1988a), it became evident that teacher appraisal was a great threat because teachers felt they were being appraised as 'people' as much as they were as professionals. Extricating the role teachers play from who they are as people, is vital if they are to become proactive and reflective in terms of their role, as it will allow them to step outside in order to look within. Just because a teacher has a bad day, it does not mean they are a 'bad' person, simply a professional with a role complexity worth exploring in as objective a way as possible. This objectivity is also necessary when investigating children's abilities, and it is to these that we now turn.

## Children's abilities

The concept of 'ability' is one which has pervaded education for many decades now, with children being labelled 'bright' or 'slow' as a consequence. The idea that ability is somehow fixed has been consistently challenged and the prevailing views have now become rapidly divorced from this trend and moved towards Bruner's (1960: 54) notion that 'any subject can be taught effectively in some intellectually honest form to any child at any stage of development'. What is needed is the recognition of where the child is and whether, by Vygotsky's (1978) terms, we are able to recognize the child's 'zone of potential development', the stage in which, with a little support, the child can make progress. This offers a balance between the curriculum and child-orientated standpoints argued earlier, because it is likely that several children can be identified who, with support, can make inroads into new learning together.

It also moves teachers away from what Alexander *et al.* (1989) and others have dubbed a 'deficit' model of teaching and learning, in which children's problems have received more focus than their potential for learning. Home background, social class and many other factors have been seen by teachers as being responsible for a child's difficulties, for example, in language performance. However, many studies, including those of Tizard and Hughes (1984) and Hughes (1989) with young children and their families, refute this and point out that children's inabilities to show competence in the classroom may be more a consequence of the way learning is presented to them and the content of interactions with the teacher than of any lack of ability on the child's part or poor parenting. Hughes (1989: 155) concludes: 'it may not matter so much whether the teacher can actually locate a specific context that brings out the best in a particular child, but merely that she believes that such a possibility exists'.

Chapter 3 includes an examination of the effects of teacher expectations on children's learning opportunities. The intention of the final activity is to investigate how a balance could be achieved for one child bearing in mind that he is one of a class of 30 children.

---

ACTIVITY 4

Having read about Sammy, rewrite the following teacher's notes indicating how you would report a more balanced view of the child under the headings given and what learning intentions seem appropriate.

SAMMY B AGED 7 YEARS and 2 MONTHS

*Social*: Sammy is very immature, chewing his fingers and sulking whenever he finds his tasks a bit difficult. Constantly seeks attention and has to be told everything at least three times! Tends to be a work avoider – he would rather play games than get on with his work. He relates well to Asmal and Ricky and plays with them outside school. It is a pity that their motivation for work, particularly maths, doesn't rub off on Sammy!

*Reading*: Sammy is slightly below average and is the slowest of the six in the middle group who read to me twice a week. He has usually lost his book when it's time to read and he gets through far fewer scheme books than the rest of his group.

*Maths*: Poor – he struggles even in the bottom group and has little idea of number bonds to 10. He likes playing in the class shop and favours this to his maths workbook.

*Parent interview*: Only mother came. She clearly feels that there is no problem. She says he is happy to read to her at home and enjoys comics, plays board games with his older sister and helps his dad on a Friday night and Saturday morning with the money collection on his milk round.

---

Eysenck (1990: 4) feels that teachers should realize that both intelligence and social class are less important than personality in determining how children approach learning and that teachers should group for personality traits. From his researches, he found that children of unlike personality such as anxious/not anxious, worked better to produce learning (p. 8). This is clearly linked with the idea of learning styles already mentioned in this chapter, to which we will return later in the book.

## Drawing the strands together

It has only been possible to open a very few doors into teachers' thinking in this chapter and all the principles identified will surface again in succeeding chapters to form the basis of ideas and suggestions for making the classroom a sound learning environment. By giving some cameos of classroom life and raising the many issues of teachers' philosophies, beliefs and values, it permits an opening for discussion through which teachers can reflect on the many facets of their role and recognize what they are currently *achieving* and the interesting challenges which face them.

Effective teachers (identified from a number of sources in both Britain and the USA) appear to have many laudable characteristics, and those which relate in particular to the dialogue on classroom organization and management include:

- creating a suitable atmosphere for learning which is positive and consistent;
- thorough planning and preparation of curricular frameworks and progression;
- using a variety of methods of whole class, group and individual teaching;
- systematic organization of resources and materials;
- having a classroom ordered for curriculum needs;
- having well-established classroom routines;
- varied presentation of tasks and activities;
- lively teaching personality;
- making efficient use of time;
- establishing high standards of presentation of self and classroom;
- animated and clear presentation of tasks with good pacing and flow;
- clarity of learning intentions and sharing these with children;
- giving helpful feedback to children on their learning and helping children to evaluate themselves as learners;
- encouraging children to be self-sufficient and learn for its intrinsic motivation;
- having high expectations of all children as regards both activities and behaviour;
- matching learning to children's needs and using observation and assessment to inform planning;
- synthesizing and analysing teaching/learning theories and classroom practices;
- regular evaluation of teaching and the learning environment.

Because the manifestation of teachers' philosophical beliefs and values occurs in this actual translation into classroom practice, it is useful to summarize briefly the main points discussed herein, in order to reflect on these when considering decisions about the physical context in Chapter 2.

In essence, teachers need to establish and maintain a balanced perspective on the many polarizations and extremes in education in order to ensure quality learning provision for all children. Such a view requires a recognition by teachers of the balance between:

1 Dealing with individuals, yet working towards meeting all children's basic educational needs.
2 Sustaining teaching and learning intentions/curriculum objectives, yet responding to children's interests and motivations.
3 Inevitably teaching through their own preferred style of learning, yet recognizing and providing for children's similar and alternate learning styles (relating to both personality and development: see Chapter 3).
4 Being the teacher, yet acknowledging one's own learning role and the need for negotiation with the children in relation to teaching and learning.
5 Acknowledging subjective beliefs about children, yet being prepared to acquire objective evidence of learning competency in school and beyond.
6 Supporting children, yet not allowing the development of unnecessary and inappropriate dependency.
7 Being prepared to teach through a variety of strategies when appropriate to learning intentions, yet allowing children to learn through practical discovery.
8 Having conviction about what one is doing, yet being flexible enough to acknowledge that which requires reappraisal.
9 Retaining the teacher's ownership and oversight of classroom activities in general, yet recognizing children's ownership over learning tasks (particularly within group work).
10 Complying with legislated curriculum requirements, yet providing and initiating relevant and purposeful activities for children.

One could also add, having a balanced perspective between the good days and the not so good!

# 2

# *The learning environment: Organizing the classroom context*

The physical environment provides both opportunities and constraints. A classroom base, containing as it does a certain amount of space, a set of furniture and fixtures, power points, windows and other light sources, teaching and learning resources, expendable materials and other bits and pieces, commands immediate attention. Organizing this range of possible teaching and learning materials, apparatus and resources requires of primary school teachers a very high level of organizational ability unique in the world of work. For the 30 or so children arriving at the start of the term, it will be their 'home' for a significant portion of each week and, as Kyriacou (1991: 76) states, 'The general appearance of a classroom indicates to pupils the care that goes into providing them with an environment which is conducive to learning.' Periodic revision and maintenance of the system created (described in Chapter 7) will ensure that the organization meets the existing and on-going demands of teachers and children.

However, a distinction needs to be made between the very evident skills of the primary teacher in the actual physical organization of the classroom, the intentions for doing it and the management structures then required. As an example, creating a classroom where the materials are arranged in a very logical way by the teacher and labelled clearly will not ensure in itself that children are able to use them effectively. As Lewis Carroll (1948: 11) wrote of the unnamed crew member hunting the *Snark*:

He had forty-two boxes, all carefully packed,
With his name painted clearly on each.
But, since he omitted to mention the fact,
They were all left behind on the beach.

It is necessary, having organized the classroom, to share intentions
and requisite strategies for access and retrieval with the children
and others who need to know. Although seemingly obvious, it is
surprising how often children in the classroom have no idea how
or why things are organized and managed as they are. If this is
also to be their learning environment, then such information is a
basic requirement, as children must be made responsible for the
equipment if they are to value and conserve it.

Particularly significant to this chapter is the need to balance
thoughts about what is essentially the teachers' domain – the classroom (for it is they who determine how it should be organized and
function) – with the needs of the children to feel it also belongs
to them. As Entwhistle (1988: 249) points out, 'the effectiveness
of learning depends ... on the situation in which learning takes
place. And the situation is the prime responsibility of the teacher.'
Yet frequently, the significantly poor state of many school buildings
and individual classrooms is highlighted in the media (see, e.g.
Purchon, 1991).

This chapter constitutes a very practical exploration of the
classroom setting. Each area identified in the main triangle in Fig.
I.1 (Introduction) is explored in turn. Aspects will be expanded
and intentions reinforced in Chapters 3 and 4 in examining provision for children's learning.

## Physical context

So, what exactly have we got in the way of a class base, ignoring
for a moment the movable components? Is the room essentially a
square, a rectangle, an L shape? Does it have alcoves, an in-built
storage area, differing floor levels? What actual floor space does
it occupy? How are the doors and windows located? What are the
other fixed and permanent elements, such as sinks, noticeboards
and permanent storage space? Is it a separate unit or will it require
access for other classes to be maintained?

Whatever the answers, however desirable or undesirable, that is
the class base, so it it vital to make the best of what exists and not
expend mental energy on 'if onlys'! However much space, we can

always do with more: windows offer light but also draughts; doors offer access but also limit use within their vicinity; stock cupboards offer storage space but also dumping grounds; sinks offer water on tap but also leaks and splashes – yet more evidence of balancing classroom needs!

A fairly large plan, however roughly drawn, helps to both confirm the mental process of 'seeing' the room and memorizing its overall capacity and provides opportunities for trying out various arrangements. The plan need only include those items which are fixed or immovable and the mobile furniture should be either stacked in the middle of the room or, better still, outside the classroom area for the time being so that a full sense of the classroom space can be gained. Figure 2.1 is a scale version of a typical plan and offers the basis for thinking about what this room has to offer in the way of space, how it may be used and the links with teaching and learning intentions.

*Space*

Particularly in a classroom new to the teacher, the next task has to be the identification and listing of everything which is occupying the space. This is time-consuming, but will reap rich rewards in the long term because the list, like the plan, can always be to hand, even outside the classroom, when planning activities and considering necessary physical and material needs. (There is enormous frustration in spending an entire evening making a language or maths game only to find, a short time later, that there was a very similar one in a cupboard all the time!) Subdivisions into furniture, furnishings, commercial and teacher-made resources and expendable materials (e.g. paint brushes, paints, sewing materials, pencils, rulers and so on), render the list more accessible. Even teachers for whom the classroom is familiar may welcome the list as a reminder of what is available and may also use the process of compiling it as part of an evaluation exercise. Most schools require staff to undertake a stocktaking exercise periodically and the list is invaluable for that purpose. If the list of resources is further subdivided into the nine main curriculum areas (usually only eight in reality because P.E. equipment in most schools is centrally stored and used), gaps in provision will become obvious and can be remedied when the opportunity arises. Figure 2.2 indicates the potential contents of such a list, but teachers should develop their own as items will vary significantly from school to school.

*Figure 2.1* Basic classroom plan – all furniture/equipment removed

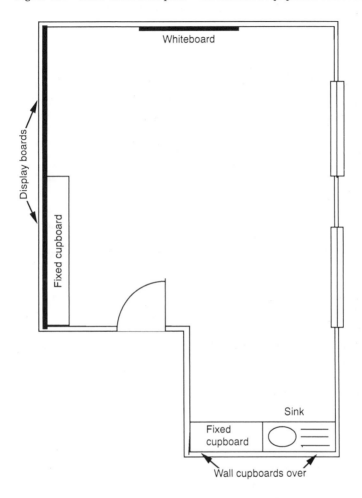

The basic practical elements sorted, we have now identified our space and equipment, but the more complex decisions about intentions for their organization require focus. Leaving aside resources, materials and furniture (to be dealt with in the next sections), how the space is to be utilized will depend on the teaching and learning styles to be promoted, as discussed in Chapters 1 and 3, and how the curriculum is to be implemented. As Alexander *et al.* (1989: 254) state: 'policy, classroom layout and practice need to be kept in step'. In an ideal world, children would be involved

*Figure 2.2* A basic list of resources and materials. How would you begin to organize them? What would be your rationale?

| Resources: | Materials: |
|---|---|
| Lego | Pritt sticks and other glues |
| Set of toy vehicles | Pencils |
| Fisher-Teknik | Coloured pencils |
| Jigsaws | Elastic bands |
| Microscope, lenses, magnifiers | Plasticine and clay |
| Display charts – various | Felt pens |
| Books – fiction | White paper – all sizes |
| Books – information | Craft knives |
| Dictionaries – various | Wax crayons |
| Snakes and ladders/other games | Coloured papers – all sizes |
| English textbooks – varied | Rulers and metre rules |
| Maths textbooks | Scissors |
| Compasses | Sand |
| Set squares | Sellotape and masking tape |
| Science all around us cards | Powder paints – various |
| Maths scheme | Readymix paints – various |
| 3 different reading schemes | Paint brushes – varied |
| Dominoes | Carbon paper |
| Tape-recorders | Spatulas |
| Musical instruments | Sewing needles and pins |
| Computer | Palettes |
| Unifix cubes | Cotton threads |
| Tape measures | 'Found' materials |
| A hamster and a guinea pig | Newspaper and magazines |
| Stopwatch and timers | Fabrics |
| Cooking utensils | Plastic tubing |
| Teacher-made materials – lots | Corks |
| Woodwork bench, wood/tools | Beads |
| First-aid box | String |
| Set of weights and scales | Straws |
| N.C. documents – lots! | Plastic sheeting |
| Sand/water tray | Glass bottles |
| Listening centre | |

in these processes, but the practicalities of this on the first day of term with a new class mean that it must be the teacher's decision, albeit to be shared with the children as soon as practicable (and amended as necessary).

Intentions to undertake whole class teaching require decisions to be made as to how this can be achieved. Many primary teachers prefer to have the opportunity to bring the whole class together on to a carpeted area rather than talk to the children when they are seated at tables. To a certain extent, this will depend on space, as it may be that providing a table and chair for every child will deny space for a carpet. The converse and regularly raised argument is that of whether a table space and chair for every child is absolutely necessary. This will equally depend on the teacher's personal preferences and the age of the children: large 10-year-olds are unlikely to relish being squashed together onto a relatively small carpet and to provide a large enough area would often leave no space for any tables and chairs! Most primary children do, however, like opportunities for working on the floor, and so this needs to be borne in mind. If the teacher is going to work with the whole class from a whiteboard, blackboard or other focal point, then the location of the carpet or the seating arrangements must enable all children to see clearly from a comfortable position without unnecessary movement (Jones and Jones, 1986: 242).

Studies by Nash (1981) and Field (1980) found that the complexity of children's activities and their commitment to and concentration on tasks was much increased when classrooms were split into bays. The balance between whole class teaching and bays can be achieved provided the bays are so located and partitioned as to allow children still to focus on a particular area of the room from where the teacher can speak to everyone. This requires any partitioning to be kept at a lower level than the head of a seated child. Teachers also need to ensure that the acoustics permit all children to hear with ease and the lighting is such that the teacher is not plunged into shadow for all or some of the children: many children rely as much on facial expression and body language for cues as they do on spoken language (Neill, 1991). Particular children, for example those suffering from glue-ear (common in younger children), will need to see the teacher's face in order to take part in the communication. Bays can also offer, as we shall see later, probably the most efficient way of storing resources.

*Display*

The way the classroom eventually looks will also be determined by the availability and use of display space, and so it is worth thinking at this stage about the location of noticeboards and a display area. Low-level central displays are perfectly feasible in most rooms, even in small areas, and still allow vision across the room. Pillars are often greatly enhanced by an appropriate display, though in many classrooms, wall space may still offer the best or only display opportunity. Having few display boards or inappropriately located boards mean that it is often necessary to

*Pillars are often greatly enhanced by an appropriate display.*

provide something else. Quick and very effective display areas can be created with a number of different materials, mostly at a reasonable cost, for example:

- polystyrene ceiling tiles (often left over from decorating in either teachers' or children's homes);
- corrugated cardboard in rolls (this can either be free-standing on cupboard tops or floor, or taped to the wall);
- cork tiles (these are the most effective but more costly unless they are available as left-overs or rejects);
- plain or small-patterned pieces of carpet also make a useful hanging to which pictures, patterns or other items can be pinned

and, if strung from a broom handle or dowelling rod, need only one nail in the wall or can be hung from available pipes or beams;

- heavy wallpaper, such as the blown vinyls, can be pasted to a wall space, though this will have to be replaced fairly regularly.

Locating the best display spaces (or identifying those which command visual attention) means going out of the room and walking back in again! Only then can you decide the areas upon which the eye naturally comes to rest. Remember also to do this at different heights in order to get the child's perspective. Low-level displays can be created by deploying unused stage blocks. The quality of the display space should occupy greater consideration than the quantity. Many primary classrooms, in the name of displaying something of every individual child's activities, are totally overwhelming and almost certainly reduce concentration rather than promote it. A few carefully selected displays which are embryonic in nature, growing with the interest in the focus, are preferable, but their location needs to offer the greatest impact and they need to be changed just *before* interest wanes – otherwise, enthusiasm often wanes with them! It is as well to remember the comment of Cullingford (1991: 33) following his discussions with children:

> The general appearance of the classroom . . . and the care taken with the wall displays makes a distinct impression on the children. It symbolizes the attention that is paid to the quality of learning.

The communicational aspects of mounting displays should be remembered for they give opportunities to:

- share and respect children's activities;
- enhance children's pride in task outcomes;
- foster curiosity about the activities of others;
- consolidate class learning;
- jog children's memories about learning;
- promote discussion and provide a stimulus;
- show visitors to the class area (internal and external) the activities of the class; and
- set quality standards.

The classroom is an educational workshop and may, occasionally, become untidy like any workshop, but should essentially reflect a business-like attitude to teaching and learning. Equipment

'The general appearance of the classroom ... and the care taken with the wall displays makes a distinct impression on the children' (Cullingford, 1991: 33).

of all kinds should be kept in good order, for we cannot place expectations of orderliness and neatness upon children if they work in an environment which has the obverse characteristics.

## *Light, heating and acoustics*

Other factors which will affect the ambience of the room for teachers and children are:

1 *Light quality*: do all the lights work? Are windows clear of obstructions? (Daylight offers quite different qualities to a room than artificial light.) Are there any dark corners which may need additional light or which can be utilized for other purposes, e.g. a stimulus area like a cave?
2 *Heating*: does it work? Is there a thermostatic control? Does the classroom have a thermometer (the normal indoor comfortable working temperature is about 20°C). Where are the sources of heat located? Do the windows open for ventilation and have you got the requisite gadget? (Red-faced, puffing children, usually mean inadequate ventilation – or playtime just gone!)
3 *Acoustics* are also a consideration, but as these change significantly once the room is full of furniture and furnishings, people and clothing, they are best tested when the room is occupied.

## Resources and materials – A place for everything and everything in its place!

In a study by Weinstein and Woolfolk (1981), 10-year-olds shown slides of classrooms, rated neat classrooms far more highly than messy ones as environments in which they would like to work. This sense of order is implicit in the general development of primary children and is worthy of attention (Cullingford, 1991). Often, the desire for order is contradicted by children's seeming reluctance to put things away but, nevertheless, knowing where everything belongs and that everything has a place is at least the basis for an orderly environment for everyone.

The problem with the primary classroom is that, of necessity, the kind of resources and materials to be found are potentially very messy! Even six jigsaws, each with 50 pieces, is a great many bits to be scattered or go missing. The coding of these will be discussed later, but a basic decision needs to be made as to general location of all resources and materials. The term 'resources' is used to include all those commercial and teacher-made items which

*A place for everything and everything in its place!*

each class usually possesses, some of which may occasionally be replenished from centralized resource areas; 'materials' denotes the expendable items – paper, pencils, paints, and such like – which require relatively frequent replenishment. It is worth saying at this point, though it will be discussed later, that a majority of resources and materials need to be readily available for children, teachers and others in the class at most times and that training in their collection and return must be undertaken early in the school year.

How resources and materials should be organized depends on a number of factors, but the most important decision is undoubtedly which type of storage is going to be most efficient for everyone. Few classrooms have perfect storage facilities and compromises will always be needed. A major question to be asked at this setting-up of the classroom stage, however, is whether resources and materials are best stored under subject headings or in a more cross-curricular way. Children have been found to use resources more effectively when materials are logically ordered and immediately to hand rather than needing to be fetched (Nash, 1981). Assuming an arrangement of bays, discussed shortly, it is reasonable that such bays will also form the basis for storage purposes.

A decision to organize resources under subject headings – maths, science, English/language, foundations and, because of the many practical resources, a combination of art/design/technology – is useful in a variety of ways:

 (i) Children begin to recognize and use the terminology which teachers now so much take for granted.
(ii) There is a by-product of this: the evidence from my own classroom is that children will then use these descriptors at home and parents gain a sense of confidence in the teacher's curriculum planning (whether this is an indicator or not, of course!).
(iii) Resource location can be explained fairly simply to children and they can learn very quickly necessary access, storage and retrieval strategies.

Balanced against these are the following disadvantages:

(a) Providing for play and topic opportunities cuts across subject boundaries and may require another area of the classroom to be assigned for this purpose.
(b) The class space and storage may be insufficient for such a wide number of different areas to be reasonably allocated.
(c) Potentially impractical working arrangements – if all the class happen to be doing maths simultaneously (advocated in Chapter 3), they may decide to converge on the one resource location at once.

I have suggested elsewhere (Moyles, 1991: ch. 4) that a useful way of considering the organisation of the classroom and its resources, given the relatively small amount of space available in most class bases, is to have no more than three main areas identified with contents further divided into subject categories if space and furniture permit. The areas could be labelled (even nominally):

• *Investigation area/bay*: essentially science, maths, technology.
• *Language area/bay*: mainly English, history, geography.
• *Creative area/bay*: mostly art, design, music.

It may be that these areas could be labelled blue area, red area and yellow area rather than using 'value' titles and the resources therein colour-coded to fit the particular bay. Whatever titles are used, explanation must be given to the children: as they develop an understanding of the classroom system, they should be encouraged to suggest alterations to make it more efficient.

An arrangement into three areas or bays retains all the advantages identified in points (i)–(iii) above and offers a solution to at least points (a) and (b). The teacher will have opportunity and space to work with a potentially large group of children (up to a third of the class) on a particular curriculum area or aspect of the topic or allow children to work independently or collaboratively with resources and materials to hand. In addition, as Wilkinson (1988: 70) points out, 'learning bays permit the maximum use of outside edges of the room', allowing greater free-movement space between the furniture. Access to materials (see above) is a management issue which will be covered later in looking at movement around the classroom.

Returning to our classroom plan, where should these three bays be located? Creative area activities with clay, paints, fabrics, glue, etc., require a location well away from any carpets or heavy human traffic and are best located by the sink (or nearest access to water). Because the investigation area may also require access to water, this should occupy the next bay so that materials can be readily gathered by the children. The language area, with its potential for quiet independent or group reading and discussion activities, is probably best located on the other side of the room. Our nominal plan may now look something like that in Figure 2.3. At present, we still have not made decisions about cupboards or other furniture for storage because the siting of these is dependent upon the quantity and type of resources finally located to each of the three bays. However, mobility of dividing 'furniture' is vital, as learning bays may need to change their shape and space periodically.

In our preparations for the children's arrival, our task now becomes one of sorting the actual resources and materials into roughly 'investigation', 'language' and 'creative' categories, a relatively simple matter given that we have already compiled the list previously discussed. Certain resources will undoubtedly 'fit' into more than one category (where should the Lego go?) and this will necessitate certain decisions. Probably, the easiest solution is to put such items where they will be most used, at least in the early part of the term, or where there is likely to be the greatest unused space. Multi-purpose resources such as the computer and tape-recorders have their locations determined by the availability of power points, unless the school is prepared to invest in extension leads and ensure these are used with safety in mind. Extension leads, where these are necessary, need to be of sufficient length to run behind, under or neatly across the back of relevant furniture (taped down to prevent them being accidentally caught up with anything else) rather than being strung across the floor. A point sometimes also forgotten, is that all cables, whether the basic ones or extensions, should be checked periodically (once a term at least)

*Figure 2.3*  Basic classroom plan – three main bays allocated

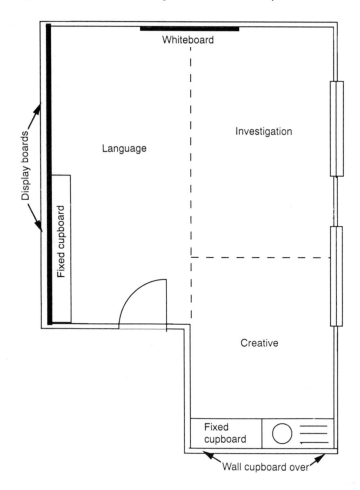

to ensure there is no wear and that each end of any cable is securely fixed to the equipment or plug.

## Coding resources with many bits and pieces

Resources like games and jigsaw puzzles have the disadvantage of having many pieces, the loss of only one of which often renders the equipment of diminished usefulness. It is absolutely essential to code each item *and* to list within the lid, base or on a separate card what the pack should contain. Teachers can do this prior to the children arriving or keep it as a purposeful task for children to do early in the term. The latter has the advantage that children will gain this sense of ownership over the classroom resources and be more persuaded to look after them. Working out the relevant classification mark is a very useful educational enterprise for children which they normally relish. The children who do the classifying and marking could also be made responsible for periodically checking their entirety. Plastic boxes (ice cream containers and the like, wonderful for long-lasting storage) can be written on with permanent spirit-based pens such as those used for overhead projectors.

## Materials

Some materials will now inevitably still be without a particular location. Will children be required to look after their own individual pencils, crayons and perhaps rulers? Developing children's sense of personal responsibility is clearly vital, but it is equally a responsible and autonomous act for each child to collect and return pencils and other items from one or more central locations. This arrangement has the advantage of offering the teacher immediate feedback on the current condition and quantity of such materials. Time is wasted by children in having to hunt for lost materials (and by teachers in having to 'nag' about them!) and central classroom storage allows opportunities for either party to keep a check. Similarly, scissor and pencil blocks (commercial or home-made from thick polystyrene or wooden blocks – a good purposeful design/technology activity!) permits the instant recognition and retrieval of wayward materials. It is expedient to have at least two locations for pencils and other basic materials, so that when class activities are undertaken children have several collection points. Sufficient pencils, crayons, scissors and rulers stored independently in small pots or blocks allow one child to collect for an entire group and minimizes unnecessary movement at the commencement of an activity.

The storage of materials can and should be made to form a learning experience in itself. The wealth of materials available in the classroom, many of which are 'found' (preferable to the seemingly less valuable label 'junk'), offer themselves for all kinds of classificatory activities for both younger and older children, as will be discussed briefly below.

*Paper and art materials*

Each area also requires its own paper storage facilities, mainly because different activities will have varying needs. Large paper storage is much more likely to be necessary in the creative bay, which, if possible, needs A1-sized shallow shelves or a plastic A1 paper tub. If the classroom has a main storage cupboard or recess, it is better to keep the larger stocks of paper there, topping up the paper locations in the bays each week as necessary. The investigation bay is likely to need a range of different kinds of papers and cardboards, such as blotting paper, tissue, cellophane and so on, and A4 stationery boxes duly labelled and stacked are useful for storing smaller-sized pieces. Larger paper or cardboard sheets need to occupy the kind of shallow shelves or tubs described above but, failing these, may simply have to be laid flat on a suitable surface with thin sheets of wood or very thick card between the different types to facilitate access to those items lower down the pile. Straight-sided plastic buckets (some come 'free', having contained chemicals like floor tile glue and been cleaned out) provide a similar storage, if not so large, as the plastic paper bins and obviate the need for lifting heavy stacks of paper. They also have the advantage, if stored on the floor, of being readily accessible even to younger children. The language bay may essentially need only A3 and A4 paper much of the time, and plastic or wire office in-trays (now available in both A3 and A4 paper sizes) stacked one above the other offer maximum space in the trays while using minimum space on top of tables or cupboards. The classroom may also have a suitable smaller drawer unit or, failing any of these, strong grocery boxes cut down in tray shapes, bound with tape to strengthen the edges and then painted with left-over gloss paint (this can also provide opportunity for colour-coding!), make very easy storage. These can be stacked on top of each other at right angles so that it is easy to see what they contain or when supplies are getting low.

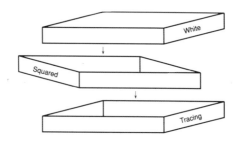

To save time and waste, it is extremely useful to have a set of papers cut to size: if A3 is trimmed by a centimetre or so on a guillotine before it is written, drawn or painted on, the full-size A3 can be used as a mount without trimming and without waste of paper. The same, of course, applies to all other sizes. This has the advantage that even young children can collect a full-sized sheet and do their own mounting and, as the paper can be trimmed in batches, it is time-efficient. The resultant 1- or 2-cm strips are useful for weaving, measuring, plaiting, labelling and a host of other purposes.

Specialist papers of any kind, e.g. foil papers or others which tend to be expensive, may need to be kept by the teacher in order to ensure economy in use. This aspect will be discussed with the children as the year goes on and can, indeed, become part of a purposeful maths activity – like the inadvisability of cutting a small circle out of the centre of a large felt square!

Crayons, particularly wax crayons, are better stored in separate colours. This surmounts the problem of the lighter colours always being streaked with bits from the darker colours, a phenomenon which aggravates children when they want to draw white clouds or snow. It has a deeper purpose, however, in that children who are drawing a picture must think before collecting the coloured crayons of their choice, deciding on the kind of colours they are trying to reproduce. They may still represent people with purple hair, but at least they have carefully selected the colours to do this rather than taken the first one they come to in the pot! If pastels and chalks are also similarly available in single-colour pots, this gives children the opportunity also to decide upon different textures within the drawings.

Yoghurt, cream and margarine tubs all make useful storage for pencils and crayons but, unless painted with gloss paint, are very weak and frequently cause disruption in class when they split when being carried across the room by a child and disgorge their contents all over the floor! A really strong set of utensil pots can be made from the inner roll of carpets or other floor coverings and are freely given away by do-it-yourself stores. Sawn through at roughly 6-inch intervals, they then only require a stiff card circle (cut from any grocery box) to be glued and taped to the bottom. They can either be emulsioned or gloss painted or covered with paper of any kind to provide an attractive and cheap storage. Several can be taped together (particularly in differing diameters and heights) to provide a composite resource for pencils, crayons, scissors and rulers.

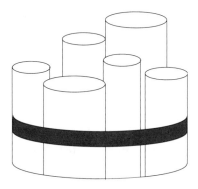

*Knives, scissors and woodwork tools*

The thought of craft knives has even experienced teachers twitching with anxiety, and it is contentious as to whether, like pointed scissors in infant classrooms, they should be readily available to children. Equated with woodwork tools, sewing needles, drawing pins and such like, children will only learn to use them properly if they are trained to do so. This is an important consideration, for if children are to be free to develop technological capabilities and their own creative ideas, they will not only need a range of techniques to be taught, but they will then need the opportunity to choose and use the material most relevant to developing those ideas. It is my contention that they should have free access to so-called 'dangerous' equipment *once they have been trained in its use.* If children are never exposed to such equipment, they cannot possibly learn how to cope with the potential safety features. An anxious, hovering adult does little to ensure children assume sensible attitudes to what is, after all, necessary learning equipment. Children should not be protected from risk but taught how to deal with it.

Anyone who has ever seen children trying to cut fabric with blunt, round-ended scissors will recognize that this is potentially far more dangerous, not to mention frustrating in the extreme, than providing training in the use and safety factors of sharp, efficient scissors to undertake the task effectively. Trying to sew with a blunt needle drives adults into despair: why do we assume it is any less infuriating for children? The big message has to be: train children in the use of such materials and then *trust them* to use them sensibly. Those who can be trusted have open use: those who cannot must prove their proficiency and ability to use appropriately in a teacher-directed activity before finally being trusted to open use. If such materials are poorly used, are the children to blame or is it that they have been given insufficient training and opportunity to show they can be trusted?

## Found materials

It is preferable to store found materials in some useful educational way, e.g. as packs of cylinders, cuboids, prisms and so on. Alternatively, found packages can be flattened for easier storage and then reconstructed *inside out* before being used for modelling, leaving an interior surface which is more accepting of poster paints than the original printed (and often laminated) cover. Found fabrics and yarns can either be stored by texture (woolly, smooth, shiny) or by colour, either way forming a useful classificatory system for children of all ages. Older children may well be able to sort the fabric by type, e.g. man-made, wool, cotton. This task can either be left to a teaching session early in the term or can be done by the teacher (or available helpers) and the system then used as a guessing game with the children the first time the materials are to be used.

## Storage of liquids

Glass jars and bottles offer the most suitable storage in that they are both strong and clear; however, they also break and create a safety problem. The large plastic sweet jars still available from some shops provide a good, large resource. Some preserved fruit now comes in plastic jars, as does syrup and, well-washed, these are strong and transparent and preferable from a safety angle, particularly with younger children. Like other relatively 'dangerous' resources, however, glass jars are acceptable provided their use is discussed with the children and provided also teachers take some steps to ensure they are kept in a suitable location. It is preferable to ensure they are stored at child height on an easily accessible shelf or on the floor in a plastic crate and that one child is allotted the task of collecting and returning them rather than everyone converging on the shelf or crate at the same time.

## Labelling

Apart from being a useful teaching point in relation to vocabulary, labelling offers all those who use the primary classroom the opportunity to find and replace items of equipment efficiently. All of us can temporarily forget where we found something, and 30 or so children are no different! At the start of the year, the location and labelling of equipment needs to be presented as a game in which all are involved and all can succeed. 'Who can find the box of Fisher-Technik materials?', or the Mobilo, the compasses, tape-measures, Logiblocks and so on. Children who locate the materials can then select a friend to try to return them to the correct place. This is quite a quick and efficient method and also means that each item can be discussed briefly with the children in relation to its use, purpose and any safety features. It is quite possible in an odd 10 minutes a day to cover most of the necessary equipment within the first week. Children must be encouraged to help each other with relocation.

With younger children or those requiring additional vocabulary activities, the teacher can write the name of the required material on a strip of paper which can then be used as a matching activity. Pictures taken from the resource packaging provide a simple, readily understood label which can also be made into a simple matching activity. Catalogues also provide useful pictures of items such as Lego, which can then be mounted on card, covered and glued or taped to the shelf on which the equipment is to be located.

All labels are better covered with clear sticky plastic as this makes them durable, particularly any labelling around the creative and investigation areas. Polythene bags, taped or stapled on, or a few coats of clear lacquer serve the same purpose. This may seem time-consuming at first, but the alternative is either constant replacement or putting up with permanently messy labels.

With the resources and materials now nominally located and labelled, it will be necessary to check from time to time on replacement needs. Have you any idea how much paper or how many pencils are used on average in a term? Children will happily accept the responsibility of stock monitoring and will readily remind teachers when supplies are low. This is particularly easily facilitated in the haberdashery shop style of having a label which details the starting amount which is then 'reduced' by the purchased amount – a very useful mathematical activity. There is nothing more frustrating than having a good idea and then not having the resources or materials for them to reach fruition.

One final point: even when children come from homes where they are expected to care for their own property and keep it in order, they will need to be 'trained' to do so effectively in the classroom and learn how to share the responsibility with others. Teachers who constantly find themselves complaining about items inappropriately replaced (or not replaced at all!) should consider whether they have actually ever discussed storage, access and retrieval with the children. Many may find they have accepted this as part of the classroom mechanisms but never shared these thoughts with the children.

## Furniture and furnishings

Furniture and furnishings are important but eminently mobile and, therefore, command less attention than the actual fixed space and the resources which, because of sheer quantity, are often more difficult to arrange. The first furniture to consider is that which provides storage. Mobile cupboard units, drawers or shelving need to be located where they are needed, now known because the resources have been sorted and allocated to a particular bay. This furniture needs positioning where it is needed and used to define the investigation, language and creative bays in, for the time being, fairly equal proportions in relation to classroom space. Where is the obvious place to locate the various materials already discussed – pencils, paper, crayons, rulers, scissors – in order to allow ready access? Have we retained display space? Have we a suitable area in which to store wet paintings, models? Are the items to which children need ready access at a suitable height for the age-group of children?

Whatever furniture you have available, it is quite likely that more than one other person in the school has a similar motley collection. It is the ideal rather than the average school which provides pristine, tailor-made furniture for, in most schools, it has been acquired over a period of time and from different suppliers. Funding for new furniture is scarce and so it is vital to make best use of what is available. Sometimes, local authorities have central stores for furniture which schools can draw on when in need and it is worth making enquiries about such services if desperate.

It is likely that you will need to move the furniture for diverse purposes during the term and so, if it will stack neatly, this will be invaluable. If you have a range of different types of chairs and tables, why not see if other teachers are in a similar position? In all probability you will find that – by asking other teachers around the school – you can accumulate at least something of a matching set of tables and chairs, even cupboards, which stand some chance of making the classroom look more uniform or having better stacking properties. If it is necessary to work within the constraints of a varied collection, then within the three bays it is worth attempting to at least have matching and stacking furniture located in each area.

Most furniture in schools is well used and its condition reflects this. If the classroom is to look attractive, the furniture may really need sanding down and re-varnishing and, in some schools, heads may already have a programme of such refurbishment in hand. Most storage units benefit from having the top surfaces either neatly painted with a coat or two of gloss or being covered with a suitable paper or cardboard, sticky plastic or polythene. Soft floor tiles or offcuts of sheeting, cork or vinyl, glued or stapled on, make an interesting and serviceable surface and can usually be acquired free from parents and other teachers. Check any such action with the head first, however.

Furniture used for storage of resources and materials may require a large amount of space, not because of the actual size of the unit, but because opening the doors requires an area to be left free in front of the unit. This may similarly apply to a stock cupboard area. Removal of the doors may be one solution. If the interior of the cupboards is suitably painted and equipment stored neatly, this has advantages in everything being visible and remembered! Some teachers may prefer to replace the doors with fabric which can give the room a more homely look, but curtains will need a periodic laundering for looks and cleanliness.

Many primary classrooms now have a carpet, so we shall assume the inclusion of a large, movable carpet. If the carpet is fixed, this feature will need to be considered earlier. In our particular classroom, thinking about whole class teaching as well as making use of the carpet for group discussions, individual and group reading and role play sessions, the carpet is best located in the central area facing the whiteboard. Figure 2.4 indicates how our classroom is progressing and now only requires consideration of the children's and teacher's tables and seating requirements.

## Teacher's table

In many classrooms, this is an object of either parochial use or piled high with the cumulative paraphernalia of many days, or even weeks. Teachers cling tenaciously to this vestige of personal territory and it is not uncommon to find the teacher's table and chair, and its attendant waiting space, occupying anything up to a third of the room. Figure 2.5 indicates this in practice on a

*Figure 2.4*   Basic classroom plan – carpet and storage units installed

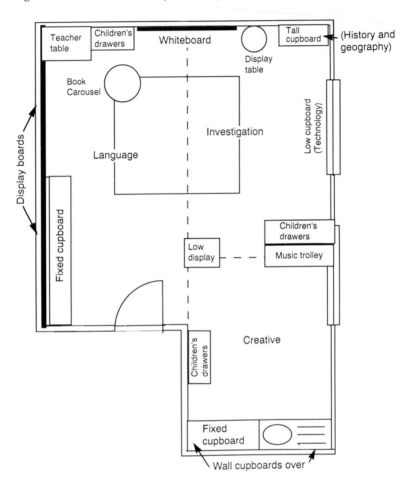

classroom plan. This arrangement implicitly both anticipates and accepts queuing by its very nature.

If teachers are truly to integrate their teaching with the children's learning, working with some groups and observing others, the function of the teacher's table requires some thought. Is it to be used for the teacher's personal belongings or for collecting items needed for whole class teaching? Will the teacher sit and mark children's work from the table or is there a more efficient system which will not lead to long queues of children? Will children place

*Figure 2.5* A furniture arrangement which both implicitly anticipates and accepts queuing by nature of the space around the teacher's area

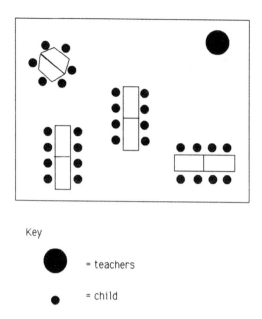

Key

= teachers

= child

their finished tasks on the table – in which case is there not a better storage area available in the classroom? A 'finished work' tray centrally located may well be preferable with the teacher commenting on completed tasks in the general round of the classroom. Are children really dependent upon that tick or do they know only too well when they have completed tasks satisfactorily? Ticks can just become one feature of the dependency model discussed in Chapter 1.

In reading stories or talking to the whole class or group from a carpet area, teachers may need a low chair from which to approach the children at a more familiar level. Siting this for easy vision across the rest of the class may be important in the early stages with a class before trusts are built up, and individual consultations with children are also possible from this position without losing a 'feel' for the rest of the class activities.

## Children's seating and work spaces

It is, of course, up to personal preference, but Cullingford (1991: 36–7) is probably correct when he suggests, from talking to children about classrooms, that they 'like their own particular part of the classroom, their seat, their view, and the table at which they can congregate with their friends'. This could be difficult to resolve if flexibility to work in different bays is required and necessitates just such negotiation with children as was previously discussed. They can choose a place in which they prefer to sit, but for some of the day they must accept that they may need to use another area of the classroom and occupy another seat – all perfectly reasonable and unlikely to wreak any kind of havoc once discussed.

The kind of seating arrangement which requires children to face each other around a large table space will promote opportunities for discussion and group collaborative work. Alternatively, it can just provide for distraction rather than concentration and confrontation rather than cooperation. Teachers need to reflect on what it is like to be in such close proximity to other people, perhaps for most of the day, in order to understand something of the seating dynamics of the primary classroom. In particular, those children whose concentration span is brief may well work more conscientiously in smaller groups or at tables around the perimeter of the room. The latter has the added advantage of freeing floor space and enabling movement around the classroom, but has the disadvantage of making whole class teaching from the child's seat base potentially more difficult. Grouping for learning will be considered in Chapter 4.

The thorny problem of desks or tables abounds with pros and cons: desks provide an immediate storage space for children's belongings without the need for additional lockers or drawers. However, even when flat-topped (and many are, of course, sloping), they make activities involving loose materials, (e.g. paint, water, glue pots, yarns, fabrics, etc.) difficult to organize, for someone will always want to get inside the desk top when the whole lot has been set out! Tables are more mobile and stackable and, despite needing drawers or lockers for children's own items are, on balance, more preferable, as they offer greater flexibility in all ways. If desks are all that is available, it may be better to attempt to provide children with alternative storage for personal possessions, e.g. drawers, lockers or even named bags (similar to plimsoll bags). It is always possible to negotiate with children, particularly older ones, to bring in only *small* personal possessions.

Storage of school items such as workbooks may be more convenient in class trays or boxes according to their topic – either specific subjects or theme focus – and advantageous in providing ready access for the teacher (for assessment or other purposes) without the necessity of hunting through individual desks or drawers. This system also tends to keep the books in better condition, as personal drawers are frequently used by children to store half-eaten crisps or apples and rarely provide clean, tidy storage. Like pencils and other materials, teachers and children should develop a distribution and collection system for workbooks from a central location. An alphabetical storage system for books is another of the useful educational devices which also serve a profitable organizational and management purpose. The relatively cheap stacking plastic crates now readily available are invaluable, though the versatile grocery box can be utilized (covered or painted and taped around its edges for strength), with cardboard separators for either system.

## Shelving

By its very nature, shelving is frequently underused in many classrooms, particularly where shelves are quite far apart in height. If stacks of equipment on shelves get too high, problems arise in extracting the bottom item. With deep shelves or underneath counter tops, and where storage is at a premium, it is worth considering suspending plastic buckets or thick cardboard soap-powder boxes (painted or covered) on hooks beneath. Dependent upon size – and many different sizes are readily available – these are useful for a wide variety of items and locations.

## Space for wet paintings and models

Being a very active environment with rather 'productive' children, there is always the problem of where to store specific items such as wet paintings and models of various kinds. Most classrooms do have some usable surface for pictures and models, but teachers need to be rigorous in ridding cupboard and counter tops of unnecessary clutter – if they do not, it is unlikely anyone else will. Neither should these be allowed to become dumping-grounds: if on-going work is to be valued, then the surface on which it rests should be labelled as to its purpose and what it is appropriate to place there, so everyone (including the caretaker and cleaners) will be clear of the intentions. Hinged wire painting racks are a very good space-saving resource, but they are costly. 'Washing lines' strung across relevant parts of the classroom, particularly over sink areas, are cheap and effective for paintings, provided drips are accounted for with polythene or newspaper coverings. An effective stacking system for paintings can also be made by

*Figure 2.6*   Simply made, cheap small shelving units

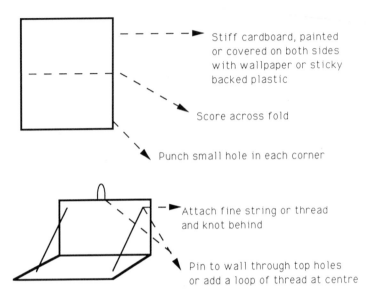

Stiff cardboard, painted or covered on both sides with wallpaper or sticky backed plastic

Score across fold

Punch small hole in each corner

Attach fine string or thread and knot behind

Pin to wall through top holes or add a loop of thread at centre

having available a pile of polythene sheets cut to a size slightly larger than the largest sized paper likely to be used, which children are then trained to interleave between the paintings: placed flat, these stop paintings sticking to each other, though if the painting is very wet, may make it liable to smudges. A display board, covered in polythene or washable wallpaper, at a convenient height and located near the creative area, allows children to hang their pictures by the corner, with either a pin or Plasfix, and occupies relatively little space. Small cardboard models can also be stored in this way, with one edge directly pinned to the board. Heavier models, for example those made of clay, need an area of shelving, though it is possible to make small shelves out of thick cardboard (or corrugated card) which can be fixed to a display board (see Fig. 2.6). Incidentally, dress-making pins are perhaps preferable to drawing pins as at least, when dropped, the former lie flat on the floor.

## Movement

As indicated by Susan Isaacs many years ago, 'It is stillness we have to justify, not movement' in the primary classroom (in Smith, 1985: 68). It is physically necessary for primary children to move.

Children and teachers will all have a variety of reasons for needing to move around the classroom with ease and the organization of its contents should allow this to happen without undue and adverse influences on others. From the location of the furniture and equipment, will children have to move for others to get by or go to their seats? Can children move easily to gain access to and return pieces of equipment? When children need to move to the carpet area for a specific session, how can this be effected without undue noise or unnecessary disturbance? If lack of space means likely difficulties, then the management of the learning environment must take account of the organizational difficulty. For example, it may be that all necessary equipment is put out by the children or teacher on to the children's tables at the beginning of each session. Similarly, it is often better for teachers to inform children that they will go to the children rather than vice versa. Assembling at the carpet area, or within a particular bay, is probably better done by using some of the many classificatory systems teachers operate, such as all those with particular clothing types, eye colours, task undertaken, by alphabetical means according to names, and so on. Teachers' own free access all over the room is vital and they should prevent finding themselves hemmed in to one area for long periods.

All of this is, without doubt, preferably negotiated with the children, as such discussion will ensure they understand the logic and purpose of what it is necessary to achieve for everyone's good. The kind of social skills required to enable such decisions are also vital to children of this age and will not necessarily be acquired without effort on the part of the teacher to ensure such learning occurs and skill developed. The Design Council (1990) recommend the use of the classroom as a source for design technology, emphasizing it as a context, environment and system with artefacts.

Movement around the classroom is also about making best use of all the space. Once the children have arrived, it is worthwhile undertaking, perhaps with a maths group, the exercise of monitoring the use of classroom spaces and, where there is any underuse, reappraising either the usual range of activities which may need extending, or whether this area (or all of it) is a necessary feature. All those earlier considerations of balance may need to be reinvestigated if, for example, the creative area is used only periodically (evaluation of the use of bays and areas of the classroom will be considered in Chapter 7).

Movement around the classroom is also about personal space. Classrooms are quite crowded places and a sense of personal space

*Figure 2.7*   Basic classroom plan – the complete room

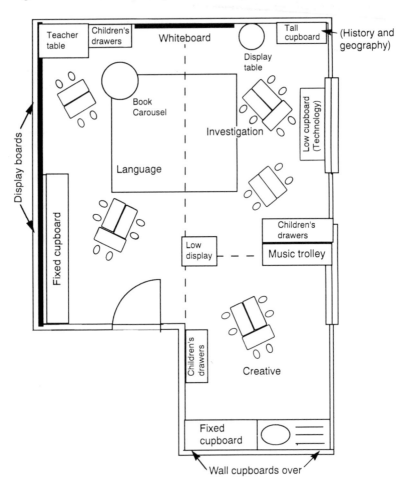

for both teachers and children needs to be created – plants in a crowded garden bed are much less likely to blossom! Drama activities which explore this notion are useful and readily translated into classroom events easily understood by children. Personal space is also about thinking time, which varies greatly between individuals.

The final version of the hypothetical classroom which has been the subject of organizational considerations is shown in Figure 2.7. The classroom described in this chapter is a combination of many types of classrooms which the writer has entered over the years. The basic organization described is possible in a wide range of settings with many different kinds of teachers and children, for its basic philosophies are compatible with a balanced view of primary education.

Further prescription is impossible for every classroom in every school is, in a variety of ways, unique. Children and their learning are the uniting factor and Chapter 3 now addresses these issues.

# 3

## The children and their learning needs: Balancing individual and whole class approaches

The importance of the first few encounters for teachers and children in establishing a positive classroom climate should not be underestimated (Wragg and Wood, 1984). Consciously and unconsciously, all those who enter the classroom will absorb factors like orderliness, noise level, atmosphere (warmth, freshness), visual appeal and general quality and, from these first encounters, will generate notions of how welcome, secure and comfortable they feel and whether they want to stay. A bright, airy, clean and ordered class base, displayed with items of interest relevant to the particular age of the children, gives the right 'feel' from the outset. Adults bringing and collecting children will equally be influenced by what they see and feel of the classroom and whether it has a sense of being geared to fostering and promoting children's learning.

The essential balance is between teachers being, of necessity, the prime instigators of decisions about the many factors discussed in the previous chapter and subsequently ensuring the children understand and can operate within the systems created. If children are to gain the most from the context, they must have some sense of ownership over the classroom and its contents. Teachers, as we have seen, tend to organize and manage their classrooms alone from their own perspectives, sharing them from the first day onwards with the children whose learning is ultimately of prime concern. (The right-hand part of Fig. I.1 in the Introduction shows children both sharing and influencing the classroom which is the focus of this chapter.)

## The children: Who are they and what are their expectations?

Children's questions about their new classroom and its inhabitants will be many, if mostly unvoiced! Will they be able to sit by their friends? Will they have their own seat and a place for their possessions? What kind of work will be expected of them and will it be hard? Will there be opportunities to play? Will they have choice? Will they be listened to when they need to know something? What will happen if they make mistakes? Is the teacher nice? Are the other children friendly? All these and many more questions will be somewhere in the children's minds during their first encounter with a new teacher in a new classroom. Whatever the age of the children, a bright and orderly classroom, where their arrival has been anticipated and their names appear prominently on drawers or listed on a board or display notice, will arouse immediate confidence in and respect for the new teacher and the new surroundings. Talking to the children at any time of the year about these aspects can be very revealing.

---

### ACTIVITY 5

Berlak and Berlak (1981: 164) point out that 'A teacher's every act signifies multiple meanings to them and to children.' *How do the children in your class feel about their learning environment?*

- Do they enjoy coming each day?
- Do they find different things to look at and sustain interest?
- Why do they think they come to school?
- What do they understand by 'learning'?
- What do they perceive as their roles in the classroom? Do boys' and girls' perceptions differ?
- What responsibilities do they *think* they have?
- What do they understand of the classroom rules?
- Can they readily find all the materials and resources they need?
- What is their perception of you as the teacher?
- What do they tell their parents about the activities of the day/ week?

---

*First encounters*

Having a name badge ready for each child (or making one as the
first event of the day) will quickly contribute to teacher and children having a contact point – the teacher should also wear a name
badge, of course. The effort spent in this kind of personalized
preparation will be doubly repaid in early relationship building
between teacher and class as well as between members of the
class. Activities which generate a cohesive feel to the class early on
are equally worthwhile, for example, children can introduce themselves to the whole class in a variety of ways:

- Shaking hands with someone they would like to get to know,
  giving their names and other information.
- Drawing pictures of themselves, pinning them up on a noticeboard and having a guessing game as to whom each represents
  (children are so much better at identifying each other's pictures
  than adults!).
- Using earlier school photographs of children with which to
  undertake a guessing game.
- Introducing themselves to another child and then having that
  child tell the rest of the class about their new 'friend'.
- The teacher may instigate a game of 'I can see someone with
  short dark hair, brown eyes, wearing a red sweater and blue
  trousers with a stripe ...', and children can try to remember
  the child's name. Once named, this child then describes someone else of their choice, and so on.
- Older children may like to interview a new friend and then
  write a biography of him or her for everyone else to read (much
  more exciting than autobiographies).
- A game where a child pretends to have something in their hand
  and tells another child their name and the name of their precious possession, e.g. 'I am Jane Smith and I have a little mouse.'
  As this goes round the class, there is much fun generated in
  trying to remember the names and possessions of, say, five
  other children and then getting together as a group to share
  what you remember.
- Older children may also like to do a collecting information
  game, where they write down on a prepared sheet information
  about a given number of other children. Those responding must
  give a different piece of information to each enquirer, so that
  at the end of the activity the teacher can ask 'Who knows
  something about Martin Jones?', and each child with information
  can read it out, building up a composite picture of Martin and
  what he said about himself. This can also become a reading

*The effort spent on this kind of personalized preparation will be doubly repaid in early relationship-building between teacher and class as well as between members of the class.*

task for younger children if the teacher has prepared some sheets of basic information (brown eyes, blonde hair, and so on) and these then have only to be ticked by the child collecting information. Writing other children's names alongside specific pieces of information on a sheet can be used for the same purpose.

*Background information*

Records passed on from the previous teachers and, unless the children are new to the school, earlier encounters will mean that not only will the teacher know something about the children, the children will also know about the teacher – if only by reputation! Both groups will, therefore, bring certain expectations to the situation and, for the teacher in particular, the more information he or she can glean about the children the better, as this will help him or her to make appropriate provision for learning from the start. Suitable learning tasks within the child's capabilities will ensure children achieve success and, therefore, recognize their own worth which, in consequence, will ensure any potential behaviour or attitude problems are averted (Westmacott and Cameron, 1988). Information which teachers will need at their fingertips, and likely to be worthwhile gathering in the days before the children start, includes:

- ages of children and age range of class;
- numbers of boys and girls (it is often said 'more boys, more noise'!);
- any existing friendship patterns among the children;
- any children with specific identified needs related to health, religion, development or learning which will require special consideration;
- any children for whom English is a second language and information about their mother tongues;
- familiarity with the contents of any pre-school assessment profile for children starting school for the first time, perhaps compiled by the parents (Wolfendale, in press);
- basic information about each child's current level and performance in core and foundation subjects – children already familiar to the school (or coming from another school) will have records or profiles from which to work;
- any topics or special interest work children have previously tackled; and
- any special talents or interests in relation to school activities.

A little later it will be necessary to consider:

- the year group to which children belong, e.g. clearly years 2 and 6 are Standard Attainment Tasks (SATs) years and it may be necessary ultimately to make special timetabling provision for these children, who may constitute only a proportion of the class or involve everyone;
- finding out from the parents or carer any significant home factors, such as children's out-of-school interests or composition of the family.

All class groups seem to have their own particular 'chemistry', teachers frequently reporting a particularly 'lively year' or a class lacking in humour and it is as well to be aware of this if the class has been together before without letting it unduly dominate thinking. Often, just the kind of cohesive start already discussed can surmount potential strife or insecurities and, in any case, children may well react and behave quite differently with another teacher in another setting. Thoughts concerning teacher expectations will be discussed shortly but first we need to consider what are the other main balances to be contemplated by the teacher regarding children and their learning?

## Necessary balances

Particularly in the early days with a new class, this balancing act is crucial for the reasons stated above and will include:

1 Being friendly towards the children, but also keeping a little personal 'distance' so as to retain clarity and objectivity about needs.
2 Being kind but firm and yet, above all, being consistent in dealing with all children.
3 Respecting children's individuality while encouraging group cooperation, mutual trust and respect.
4 Establishing quickly the patterns and routines for the children's day which will provide the background to effective communication, yet remaining flexible and sensitive to necessary changes.
5 Negotiating classroom 'rules' with which everyone agrees to conform, yet ensuring both groups are prepared to re-negotiate these when circumstances change.
6 Encouraging early independence in the teacher–children relationship while fostering a sense of unified purpose.
7 Proffering equal opportunities for all children, yet employing positive discrimination where appropriate.
8 Encouraging friendships while not permitting exclusivity of certain groups.
9 Having knowledge of the children from records but accepting that different teachers have contrasting expectations of children and that children react differently with different teachers.
10 Recognizing and acknowledging the range of backgrounds of the children and the family's role in the child's education, yet avoiding unprofitable labelling.

As life with a new class develops, this balancing act will also include:

11 Acknowledging different learning styles, yet encouraging variety in learning strategies.
12 Ensuring activities are relevant and purposeful to the children while enabling children's entitlement to a broad and balanced curriculum.
13 Acknowledging achievement and progress, yet not making children reliant upon extrinsic rewards.
14 Sustaining children's interest while working with them towards explicit learning intentions.
15 Promoting children's thinking while acknowledging that it

is qualitatively different from adult thinking – but equally worthy.

There are many overlaps here, as one would anticipate, between the balances required in relation to the teacher and teaching and those relating to the children and learning. Similarities highlight areas of compatibility between teaching and learning, while differences evidence their sometimes conflicting parallels. As an example, while bestowing praise ostensibly supports children's learning and is a pleasant point of contact for teachers and children, it can actually be quite harmful in that some children become dependent on such constant feedback, making them both reliant on the teacher for the reward and reliant upon the reward itself for motivation (Holt, 1991: 139–40). What is clearly necessary is to look beyond the immediate and superficial effects of a particular teaching or learning strategy and try to establish the causes of certain behaviours – praise may appear to make children work harder, but what was the cause of any reluctance to do so in the first place? Smyth (1990: 491) gives a related and pertinent example of a teacher's thinking about a child: 'John didn't finish his work again today. I must see that he learns to complete what he has begun.' Smyth (1990: 492) offers alternative questions about this scenario: 'Why did John not finish his work? Why should he finish his work? How does John see the tasks demanded of him? Are the tasks of the right kind, quality and quantity?' These questions suggest a very different approach which has the learner's needs rather than managerial expectations at its core and this is worth exploring, particularly in relation to teachers' expectations of children.

## A self-fulfilling prophecy? – Teachers' expectations of children

Most classes reflect a great deal about the style and expectations of the teacher; a collaborative, good-humoured teacher generally has collaborative, good-humoured children. It is also true to say that quiet teachers tend to have quiet classes, and vice versa. (If you doubt this, think about the staff in your own school.) This 'chemistry' also occurs between individuals and it is very difficult for all teachers to like all the children in their class: we are only human after all. However, we are responsible for teaching them all to the best of our and their ability, so we need to concentrate attention on finding one or more particularly positive aspects of each child from which we can form a satisfactory personal picture and build relationships. Some teachers particularly like the 'characters' in their classes, other teachers prefer children who are perhaps less creative in their approach to learning and conform more to the norms expected of a particular age group. Either way, classes will have both types and one of the skills of the teacher, discussed in Chapter 1, is that of being objective in dealing with all children.

---

ACTIVITY 6

*How does your memory of children operate?*
Without thinking too hard, begin to list the children in the class.

- Who are the first three on the list?
- Who have you forgotten?
- Why did certain children spring to mind more quickly than others?
- How do you feel about these children?
- Does this tell you anything about personal preferences?
- Is there anything you need to think further about professionally?

---

The likelihood is that teachers and children may well come from very different social and cultural backgrounds, with different value systems and child-rearing practices. Recognizing one's own preferences and biases is the first step to preventing unwitting or unnecessary stereotyping or criticism. Such balancing of personal views with professional practice was evidenced in Nash's (1973) study of primary teachers in Scotland, when it was found that the profile of particular children's performance in a class varied considerably according to the teacher's manifested perceptions of them: children perceived favourably by the teacher did well and said they liked being with that teacher, but where children did not do well, they were not favourably perceived by the teacher and reported not to like being with that teacher.

There are many other fascinating studies, a few of which are worth exploring. As you read, it may be interesting to consider how you would react in each situation and if what is said applies to any thoughts you have on children in your class. The associated teacher behaviours in relation to expectation are particularly noteworthy.

Meighan (1981) explores a number of studies of the effects on both children's performance and competence of teachers' implicit expectations and the resultant differences in approach to teaching. Harvey and Slatin's (1976) study of teachers' immediate perceptions and willingness to specify children's likely performance characteristics from being shown photographs of individuals resulted in lower-class children, particularly black children, being rated less favourably. Palardy (1969) studied American lower grade elementary school teachers over a period of time in their dealing with a class of children all from similar home backgrounds. The researcher found that those teachers who believed that (a) girls were superior to boys in learning to read or (b) thought there was little difference, had beliefs which significantly influenced the children's actual outcomes in terms of reading performance. Chaikin *et al.* (1975) found that when 48 student teachers were told that a 10-year-old boy (to whom they were to give a lesson on house safety) had high, as opposed to low, motivation and intellect, those teachers who were led to believe 'high expectancy' used different strategies for teaching. They leaned forward more, looked pupils in the eye longer, nodded their heads up and down and smiled more. Chaikin *et al.* believe that these gestures provide easily recognizable indicators of approval which can be read by pupils (albeit, perhaps, unconsciously).

Good and Brophy (1984: 104–5) cite many research studies on teacher expectation which indicate 'differential teacher treatment of high and low achievers'. This includes waiting less time for perceived low-ability children to answer, giving them answers, offering less frequent encouragement, paying less attention or interacting with them less, calling on low achievers less often to respond to questions, seating them further away from the teacher, having less friendly interaction, reduced eye contact and less non-verbal communication.

Doherty and Hier (1988, p. 345), in their study of sex differences in teacher's expectations of year 5 and 6 children, conclude:

(1) Primary school pupils who are more positively perceived by the teacher tend to receive more favourable predictions for reading and mathematics than pupils who are less favourably perceived, *even when academic competence in these subjects is controlled.* [original emphasis]
(2) Among those who are less favourably perceived by teachers, boys seemed to be especially subject to faulty predictions, particularly in reading.

(3) Teacher expectation effects may be more precisely measured when academic predictions in a specific standardized test are compared to the children's actual performance in that test.

Item (3) is significant in relation to assessment under the National Curriculum and the comparison of results between SATs and teacher assessments.

The fact that many such studies have drawn similar conclusions suggests that an awareness of children's capabilities, particularly in relation to our expectations of them, is a vital feature if children are to achieve their educational potential. Again, the point needs reiterating that teachers are continually learning in their own classrooms and beyond, in the process of reflecting on their own attitudes and approaches as well as on those of the children. In making plans for children's learning, it is essential to work from the 'facts' about children as a starting point and also to be aware of how physical gestures and facial expressions give only too evident clues to learners of the teacher's inner feelings (Neill, 1991: 146).

## What is learning? Some theories and ideas

As we have seen in Chapter 1, teachers' values relate to being competent in what they do, clear about aims and needs, consistent in approaches and responses and generally having a cool, calm and collected approach to the job of teaching. But learning and being a learner is not like that (Claxton, 1991: 129). It is uncertain, often incompetent and clumsy in the early stages, certainly inconsistent (happening in spurts and rushes depending on how we feel and what we are approaching), and unclear some of the time about where we are going until we get there. Kyriacou (1991: 68) expresses the view that 'Learning is an emotionally high-risk activity and failure is often extremely painful.' Teachers recognizing this state in themselves should take heart in the fact that they, too, are clearly learners in the classroom!

In relation to contemplating children's learning, a simple model evolves around the three propositions how, what and why:

- How do children learn and what are the variations in learning styles and strategies which can be expected?
- What should children learn in terms of content and skills and in what format?
- Why is this learning important for children; why should children

participate in the learning process and what will be their perceptions of the purpose and their role in it?

The further questions of how children may approach tasks and
with whom is the focus of Chapter 4, while Chapter 5 investigates
issues of time, the structure of the day, routines and timetabling.
   Each of the three propositions will now be discussed in relation
to the effects of classroom organization and management upon
them.


*How do children learn?*

Many theories have been postulated over the last three or four
decades in relation to children's learning which have significantly
influenced current thinking (Wood, 1988, gives an excellent com-
pilation and review of these, which teachers would find accessible). The notion of intelligence *per se* is now thought to be less
useful than considering how different intelligences are formed
through learning processes (Gardner, 1983) and the ways in which
the learning environment, in this case the classroom, can promote
children's intellectual development (Wheldall and Glynn, 1989).
   Because of the complexity and, as yet, incomplete understanding of how people learn, factors which provide the *circumstances*
in which learning takes place offer a more practical approach to
considering learning. In the classroom context, a combination of
interactionist/constructivist theories, which effectively synthesize
a range of other theories, appear to encapsulate the most useful
notions relating directly to children learning. Interactionist beliefs
are based on the pivotal notion that each of us learns, at a higher
mental order level, from others, through interacting with them in
a variety of ways and in a variety of contexts (Vygotsky, 1978) –
in this case, the school and classroom. This is really at the heart
of primary education; that it is both a social and an educational
process. Collaborative grouping of children, managed in such a
way that children are motivated and able to learn from such interaction, is a clear example of one element of this in practice. The
other main element is expressed by McAuley (1990: 89), who feels
strongly that 'the teacher–child interaction ... is at the heart of
the educational process'. However controversial it may sound, it
is undoubtedly impossible for a teacher to understand the learning
needs and styles of every single pupil in the class: as yet learning
is too poorly understood. Therefore, any such knowledge is based
mainly upon insights gained from glimpses into children's

*The learning environment can promote children's intellectual development in many ways.*

understandings: this is where the interactionist perspective links with constructivist views.

The constructivist view is most clearly expressed by Claxton (1990: 57), who explains:

> ... learning is a personal and an active process. It is personal because we can understand or retain new things only in terms of the pre-existing knowledge that we bring to the learning situation. And learning is active because it is only through the purposeful mobilization of this store of knowledge that new knowledge or skill can come about. We have no other place to stand, in order to comprehend the world, than on the platform of our own current knowledge.

Such a view encompasses the basic premise that what children bring to learning is of equal importance to what they take away from it. Galton (1989, p. 14) is of the view that the 'constructivist paradigm makes it possible to interpret such classroom events as products of a series of bargains between the teacher and pupils'.

In terms of what has already been said about the classroom as a learning environment, the two notions together form the core in relation to organizing and managing children's learning: children will learn from the teacher and each other given certain structures and systems obtaining and construct and use new knowledge from existing understandings and skills, many of which will be common among the children. The crux is that children must be 'actively' engaged in the process in a way that matches their learning style. It must be remembered that 'activity' in this context as much relates to mental action as physical action. A feature of such mental activity is in ensuring that children, like teachers, are proactive in their approach (not simply reacting to teachers' demands) and that they are encouraged to be reflective about their own thinking (Desforges, 1989). The teacher will only get to know about the children if the children can express their own learning needs.

## Learning styles

In Chapter 1, a theory of adult learning styles was postulated in relation to teachers' teaching styles. Jones and Jones (1986: 70) proffer a complementary notion of children's learning styles, suggesting four (not necessarily discreet) categories:

1 *Innovative learners*, who need personal involvement in all learning situations, who seek meaning, want reason, are innovative, and imaginative. It is suggested that these children need the teacher mainly as motivator and discusser.
2 *Analytic learners*, who want to know facts, perceive abstraction and reflect thoughtfully and who create concepts, build mental and practical models. Such learners need the teacher as informer and direct instructor.
3 *Common-sense learners*, who need to know how things work, to solve problems through hands-on experience and enjoy practical application of knowledge and skills. These learners need the teacher as a coach who will give feedback and interact in an on-going way.
4 *Dynamic learners*, who are self-discoverers, take chances, are flexible and enjoy change, seek action and follow plans. The teacher is needed as a resource, as an evaluator and facilitator.

These four learning types implicitly include the notions of visual, auditory and kinaesthetic learning styles. Put simply, many people learn mainly by actually doing things for themselves (kinaesthetic learners), whereas others absorb information and skills adequately from listening (auditory learners). A majority of learners, particularly children, require visual activities and these have the greatest impact on memory. In each case, storage and retrieval of knowledge will require the employment of different strategies, with visual learners having an immediate photographic system, auditory learners operating in sequential fashion and requiring verbal precision, and kinaesthetic learners operating at a physical level on both counts (SEAC, *c.* 1990). It goes without saying that, for example, auditory learners will need classroom conditions which permit them to hear clearly what is said, visual learners will need plenty of visual stimuli, and kinaesthetic learners greater opportunities than other children for practical activity and movement. There is also a recognizable link with the contentious brain dominance theories which relate the differing functions of the brain's right and left hemispheres to variation in learning styles, particularly, according to Moir and Jessel, (1989), in relation to boy–girl differences (discussed further in Chapter 4).

It is clear that the children in any class will be distributed across these learning style categories and it is vital, if teachers are to group effectively, that information is gained about children's learning preferences. Gathering such information will in itself need time and commitment, but these features are far more viable and require far less emotional energy than attempting to deal with factors which are beyond the teacher's control, such as socio-economic background or various potentially ill-defined notions of 'ability'. The danger is that these four learning types may themselves become 'labels' and teachers should constantly remind themselves that different curricular experiences, peer influences and availability of resources may well influence and modify children's individual learning styles.

Consider also that most children (and adults) need intermittent periods of time 'off-task' in order that subconscious learning processes are given the chance to operate effectively (Raven, 1989) – the notion of 'sleeping on a problem' is one well known for its success! In the classroom, this time could constitute 'practice' activities, which make few new learning demands on children. Children, given choice, will often choose to do those activities which constitute a rehearsal or revision of previous learning.

These different styles can also be incorporated into whole class teaching plans so as to include various elements within the session. The 'doers' among the children can be called upon to provide demonstrational points and the teacher can ensure that verbal information is accompanied by visual prompts. Davey (1983: 78) believes that for all children, teachers should rely 'less on telling out of context and more on showing within context', clearly advocating a demonstration rather than an expositional style by the teacher. Children who need interaction with the teacher can be prompted through offers from the teacher to make a contribution through questions or statements and those who need more in the way of discussion can be encouraged, by suggestion from the teacher early in the session, to think about formulating discussion points for follow-up activities. With younger children in particular, the teacher needs to stop at approximately 5-minute intervals to allow children to talk about, and therefore reflect upon and consolidate, their thoughts on the matter.

Teachers frequently isolate a particular child to answer a question. Unless the child's and the teacher's style facilitates the child's learning in this way, many children will suffer enormous embarrassment from not being able to respond through, perhaps, not yet having internalized the information sufficiently in their own inimitable way. Understanding the child's learning style will help the teacher to be more sympathetic to different children. Just think, this may be a way of legitimizing the actions of the child who just cannot help making a verbal contribution when the teacher actually feels others should contribute! It may be that some children will not readily respond in that situation because their learning style is more reflective and analytic.

## Learning processes and outcomes

As the National Curriculum has made clear, curriculum learning has four central tenets – knowledge, skills, understandings and attitudes. These will be acquired via a number of learning processes adopted through a variety of learning styles. There are, of course, many arguments as to what constitutes knowledge, let alone how it should be assessed. Knowledge based on the concepts of 'to know' clearly has several facets, one of which might be called straightforward, *factual* knowing – knowing 'that' and knowing 'what' (essentially product based) – whereas another knowledge form might be deemed to be more potential based and related to knowing 'why'. Once again, these are not polarizations; rather, they constitute an amalgam of usable knowledge. Similarly, we all need to acquire and practise certain skills to undertake day-to-day living and to develop understanding of the world about us and ourselves within it. Interpreted in this broad, balanced and relevant framework, there can be few arguments against this conception of school learning.

The notion of a sequence of learning processes (Hull, 1990: 62) is a useful one to review, for it is at the heart of the learning process. Particularly in school, it stresses teaching and learning intentions and it has outcomes which can be assessed. Learning

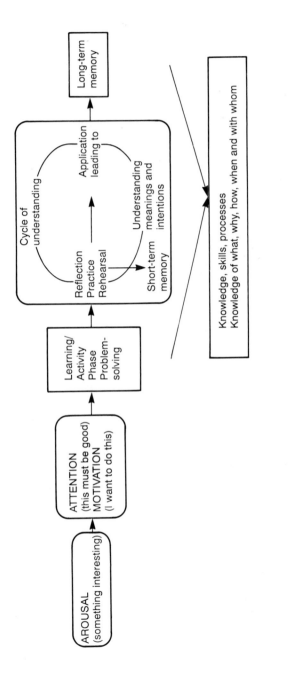

*Figure 3.1*   Learning essentially results from a combination of many factors

potentially occurs as a result of the factors shown in Fig. 3.1, with some elements requiring greater attention for some children and adults dependent upon their learning style.

There is research evidence (e.g. Bennett *et al.*, 1984), to suggest that many primary children, irrespective of learning need or style, spend undue amounts of time on practice tasks at a low intellectual level and that a balance of tasks needs to be achieved. Equally, much memorizing in school tasks is for its own sake rather than for what it will actually contribute to deeper level knowledge. The model is useful when considering the management of learning tasks for, inevitably, in any class there will be children who are at different stages in the model in relation to learning. At any time in the ongoing programme, there will be children who objectively fall into roughly three groups requiring:

1 New learning of some kind or extension of previous learning.
2 Practice, rehearsal, revision or reflection opportunities.
3 Consolidation and application processes.

There may also be one or two children who, for various individual reasons, require a specific or different activity though, on the whole, this three-way system is workable and manageable in terms of the teacher's available time and optimum learning time for children. In relation to the organization of bays and areas suggested in Chapter 2, this grouping operates effectively within that arrangement and can accommodate sub-groups within an area for curriculum or resource purposes.

Holt (1991: 25) offers a pertinent point in relation to the type of learning required in 3 above, suggesting that children have to:

> ... live with an idea or insight for a while, turn it around in some part of their minds, before they can ... discover it, say 'I see', take possession of the idea, and make it their own – and unless they do this, the idea will never be more than surface, parrot learning, and they will never really be able to make use of it.

---

## ACTIVITY 7

*How might all three learning groups operate in the classroom?*
Scenario: The children have been working on a topic about fish. So far they have:

● had a story about fish;
● had the chance to examine a real (but dead) trout;

- identified the habitats of different kinds of fish;
- drafted a poem about fish;
- produced a class database on the computer about fish; and
- begun an individual topic book on their favourite fish.

What will they do next? How much of it will be 'teacher-intensive'? How can children's previous learning be built upon? Plan some activities for tomorrow which are appropriate for the children and teacher.
(Teachers can use the example given or, preferably, work from a curriculum aspect on which they are currently embarked. Either way, teachers will need to ask how the children in their classes 'fit' this management scheme. How far are you able to take account of different learning styles in the activities provided? What information do you need to gather to help with this planning?)

---

This type of learning framework meets what Alexander *et al.* (1989) saw as necessary compromises to be made by teachers in making decisions on how to organize children into suitable teaching groups. They suggest that the major decisions to be made centre around 'what the children will learn that day, what children's learning will receive the teacher's attention at any one time, how the working environment can best facilitate that learning' (p. 263). It may also resolve something of the dilemma suggested in the work of Solomon and Kendall (1979, p. 257) in ensuring that within the class different types of learning opportunity are taken into account. Their suggestion was that

> across class types, it is possible to identify those in which high achieving children do their best and those in which low achieving children do their best; these are usually not the same types of class.

*What should children learn? The wider connotations of curriculum*

Activity 7 focused attention towards what children should be learning in one particular situation. What children should learn in schooling carries its own weighty legislation, yet much is still expressed in relation to primary education regarding 'basic skills'. Nearly always this appears, particularly in the media, to be construed as reading, writing and calculation, with some science occasionally thrown in for good measure. But as Thomas (1985: 2) suggests, basic skills in primary schooling are far more wide-ranging and cover:

- the capacity to memorize, organize and write;
- the capacity to apply knowledge (across the curriculum), do practical problem-solving tasks and investigate;
- a range of personal/social skills, e.g. the ability to relate, to cooperate, offer leadership and work alone without close supervision;
- motivation, commitment and an ability to accept 'failure' and be self-reliant and self-confident.

Downey and Kelly (1979: 22) discuss skills learning generally as 'knowing how rather than knowing that', but deem basic skills to include motor skills plus four types of skills-learning occurring within the school context which closely match those of Thomas but to which they add critical thinking skills. Rodger and Richardson (1985: 86) suggest that effective learning is seen as the integration of cognitive, affective, psychomotor, interpersonal and intrapersonal (self-knowledge) skills.

In managing children's learning, teachers will find, of necessity, core and foundation (mainly cognitive) curriculum aspects dominating, but it is relatively simple to add a column or two to typical planning sheets as an *aide mémoire* in relation to both wider basic skills and potential learning styles. There seems to be no discrepancy in principle with those curriculum aspects determined within the National Curriculum: primary education certainly cannot afford, for the sake of the children, a narrow definition of 'basic skills' or of learning. It needs to be remembered that basic skills are just those skills which we must learn in order to deal relatively automatically with various aspects of our lives. Therefore, in child and curriculum terms, many of the basic skills will need to be applied across many aspects of the curriculum and may not need to be extensively dealt with in isolation unless particular features require a teaching point. As an example, children may well undertake writing about some geographical learning in which all or some show evidence of requiring further work on grammatical aspects of writing (perhaps understanding adjectives or using contractions). This should not interfere at that time with the geographical work, which will have its own intentions, but should be noted by the teacher as requiring attention within an English activity.

In thinking about setting tasks for children, there is no better gauge of acceptability criteria than oneself. The big question is: 'Would I want to do this task myself?' If teachers think about this and give a negative response, is it likely that children will be motivated? Would you really want to sit and write your news or diary every Monday morning (especially if you had a rather boring weekend)? Faced with a page of numbers, would you really want to have to complete them all, especially if you are not really fond of numbers or paper and pencil learning and do not like the pressure of working on your own? Would you equally not wish to know when enough was enough? A diet of working through exercises gives little sense of satisfaction at completion because the task is only fully completed when the workbook is finally finished – and then another one usually follows. Many teachers will suggest that children actually like these tasks – and many appear to do so – but this may be as much related to the values teachers and parents apparently attach to such activities rubbing off on the children as to the children actually enjoying the tasks. Children, like adults, will also resist having too much demanded of them, and the constant challenge of everything being new learning may well take its own toll. Much teaching and learning could occur more effectively if teachers really identified with the tasks they present to children rather than just 'delivering' the curriculum! This also clearly relates to teachers ensuring children are appropriately challenged by some of the activities, whatever the format, and understand the learning intentions, which in turn is linked to children learning how to learn and be learners.

## Challenges in learning, intentions and learning about learning

Any models of learning which suggest a straightforward linear pattern or an equally straightforward relationship between teaching and learning, deny the fundamental complexity and affective nature of the learning process. Learning is essentially about taking risks and many primary teachers, particularly those teaching younger children, have created dilemmas for themselves in trying to protect children from so-called 'failure' situations and being 'upset' (Desforges, 1989). Paradoxically, most primary teachers have been equally ready to put ticks and crosses against children's written efforts – clear indications of being 'right' or being 'wrong' without evidence for the children, or the teacher, of how and why such errors have occurred (another example of unhelpful polarizations). Yet the most effective learning incidents include making mistakes, acknowledging the difficulties and gaining understanding of both consequences and how things could achieve a level of success. Because of perceived pressures of time, teachers are often unwilling themselves to take risks, preferring to work within the known and, therefore, are models of a no-risk-taking attitude for children. Most exciting learning, however, is about risk-taking and being wrong; in fact, children and adults do this all the time in the world outside school, anything remotely inventive having gone through several error processes, analytical discussions and evaluative sequences before acceptance. Having arrived at that point, further possible innovation or extension may well come to light – just consider the case of computers and how far they have come in 30 years or so! No such developments are possible without people who are geared for taking risks and are open enough to new learning to accept it as a challenge rather than as a threat (see Dennison and Kirk, 1990). How far do schools really educate children for this kind of thinking and learning? Is it possible to do so within whole class teaching or is this a highly individualized way of learning? How do you deal with 'error' or risk-taking in your classroom?

Children who are presented with mundane tasks and few challenges will inevitably be bored children. Cullingford (1991: 21) found that boredom is very real among the full range of primary children and that it is generally associated with 'work' (essentially written work) rather than practical activity and choice. He suggests 'The contrasts are not between hard work and "soft" but between activities they are engaged in and activities that are routine' (p. 157). There is insufficient space to go into the work/ play arguments (Moyles, 1989) and, in any case, they are yet another unacceptable polarization. Any task, however complex, can be undertaken playfully by children and adults – and still be hard work! It is a matter of what you believe you are doing which is significant and how the tasks are presented. It is necessary to acknowledge that we need to know more about what children gain through play experiences, but equally, where is the evidence that they gain any more, with any greater success, through working on low-level tasks with no cognitive, affective, psychomotor, interpersonal or self-knowledge challenges? At the very least, in play, children are motivated to practise skills and explore materials and are less likely to find alternative outlets for their energies (in perhaps disruptive behaviour) when bored by completing pages of sums they can or cannot already do, or exercises which hold little purpose for them. As Jenks and Kelly (1986: 37) attest:

'Taking orders is tedious. Making decisions is fun. Rote assignments are boring. New challenges stimulate.'

All primary children enjoy activity, peers and games (Cullingford, 1991: 124). Teaching should capitalize on this, ensuring that suitable materials are available, that children can see *purpose* in what they are doing and understand their own strategies for approaching learning. Karrby (1989: 51) found that 5- to 6-year-olds were far more able to 'recount, describe and explain in a richer way' about their own learning from engagement in play activities than in teacher-dominated learning, in the former conceiving learning in a whole way, in the latter describing it as unconnected events, with a goal of doing what the teacher wanted rather than learning. When first taught metacognitive approaches (learning about their own learning: Pramling, 1988: 277), Swedish 6- to 7-year-olds were able to quickly develop an awareness of their own learning and then use the knowledge in discussing what they had learned and reflect on the processes of their learning – clearly helpful information for any teacher. There is every reason to believe that older children gain equally from learning how to learn (Nisbet and Shucksmith, 1986). Directing questions at children in such a way as to require them to reflect on the strategies they use for gaining information or arriving at solutions can easily and quickly become part of the teacher's repertoire. They require only a shift in emphasis – instead of straight answers, children can be asked to explain the processes they went through to arrive at that point. This is far more revealing than knowing the answer and alerts teachers and children to any 'faulty' strategies being developed.

Sharing these learning about learning strategies can also be promoted in peer learning situations. Cullingford (1991: 124) says about children's preferences:

> ... of all styles of classroom organization, the possibility of working with someone else seems to them one of the most important, not because they just enjoy working with a friend, but because they feel they can receive help, give help and exchange ideas.

It is certainly the case that we learn more about ourselves in the social situation by taking notice of the responses of others in such interactions.

Common sense and a developing number of research outcomes suggest cooperative and collaborative group work is the way forward to successful, effective and efficient learning and teaching, and this will be discussed in more detail in the next chapter.

### General thoughts on organizing and managing children's learning

However poorly and inadequately we can at present define or understand learning, this must not be an excuse for doing nothing other than following blindly what is set before us or what has gone on before. Common sense and observation of children will tell us that learning goes on all the time and that we are privileged to share *some* of this with the children in school *some* of the time. Knowing the learners' needs intimately is a vital step, but getting inside children's heads is notoriously difficult: adult values and experiences mean that we interpret events very differently from children. Ausubel *et al.* (1978: 163) believe that 'The most important single factor influencing learning is what the learner already knows. Ascertain this and teach him accordingly.' In principle, most teachers would readily concur: in practice, 30 children or more make this virtually impossible. An alternative has been intimated earlier: if teachers can be persuaded to make their thinking about learning intentions more overt to children within teaching activities, then the learners will have more opportunity of relating this to knowledge and skills they have already acquired. A further positive consequence would be that in opening up their teaching in this way, it is likely that children will be prompted to generate more questions about teaching intentions and subsequently their own learning. The relative rarity of children asking learning-generating questions is evidenced in many classrooms.

As a final activity, think about a typical session in your class, your learning intentions and how they are conveyed to children by whatever process.

---

ACTIVITY 8

*How many children in your class will know (really know!):*

- What they are going to do.
- How they are to set about the task.
- For what learning outcomes are they are doing the task.
- What learning strategies they can best utilize.
- What is the most appropriate way to begin the learning.
- How they will access necessary materials.
- What usefulness the learning has to them in the present and/or future.

- When they have finished.
- Whether they have been successful.
- An appropriate way of practising any new skills.
- The potential for transferring this learning to another situation.

---

In other words, what is it like being a learner in your classroom? Teaching which builds in these aspects is more likely to be successful with all children for the variety of reasons already outlined in this chapter. Chapter 4 will now move the discussion further in dealing with issues of allocating tasks to children, grouping for learning, behaviour matters and equal opportunities for all learners.

# 4

## Grouping children for teaching and learning: Providing equal opportunities and promoting appropriate behaviour

As we have seen generally in Chapter 3, children's learning needs are many though commonalities abound. Derived partially from a list compiled by Jones and Jones (1986: 57), the following features appear to be of prime importance in ensuring primary children learn effectively. They should:

1 Understand the teacher's intentions.
2 Be actively involved in the learning process (both mentally and physically).
3 Relate subject and cross-curricular matter to their own lives and to classroom learning.
4 Follow aspects of their own interests and be encouraged to relate these to the interest of others (including the teacher – balance again!).
5 Experience success, 'failure' and learning through trial and error.
6 Receive realistic and prompt feedback.
7 Experience an appropriate amount of structure.
8 Be given time to integrate different aspects of learning.
9 Have positive contact with peers.
10 Receive teaching matched to their learning styles.
11 Understand their own learning strategies.
12 Be given opportunities to learn playfully.

13 Have opportunities to generate and ask purposeful questions and seek answers.

14 Have opportunities for interaction with a range of adults.

15 Be allowed time for reflection and proactive processes.

16 Be given time and opportunities to concentrate on and sustain interest in activities.

17 Experience a broad, balanced and purposeful curriculum relevant to their needs both collectively and individually.

18 Be able to make sense of the classroom learning environment.

Teachers who can assure themselves that these aspects are part of the experiences provided in their classrooms have indeed something on which to establish effective learning. The crucial aspects of this chapter are those concerned with how tasks are allocated to children and communicated in regard to learning, grouping, equal opportunities and behavioural issues.

## Allocating tasks

The successful allocation of tasks to class, group and individuals is dependent upon a few main teacher factors:

1 Being explicit and ensuring that children are clear about what they have to do *and why.*

2 Training children to go about their tasks in an appropriate manner – and then trusting them to do so!

3 Expecting children to undertake their activities diligently and with good-quality outcomes – and then ensuring they do through praise, displays, contact with parents, other teachers, other classes (remember, praise must be worthy, otherwise it is valueless and potentially dangerous: see Holt, 1991).

4 Expecting children to behave properly – having established what you mean by good behaviour – and reinforcing suitable behaviour by pointing it out rather than dwelling on inappropriate behaviour through constant reminders or 'nagging'.

5 Operating a system based generally on promoting children's independence and self-esteem – with opportunities to exercise it through giving elements of choice.

6 Ensuring there is sufficient challenge of varied types in the activities to interest children with different approaches to learning.

7 Providing a range of different strategies and outcomes to accommodate different learning capabilities and needs.

8 Ensuring that assessment of children's progress and attainment

*Teachers need to train children to go about their tasks in an appropriate manner and then trust them to do so!*

is used to identify common needs which will then inform future planning.

The allocation of tasks to the whole class, groups or individuals may be achieved by:

- verbal instructions – to class, groups, individuals;
- charts of various kinds indicating where children should be in terms of class area/bay or what learning they should undertake;
- task cards or task sheets;
- activity lists, all children working to their own list of tasks or children designated to tasks by identifying their name on an activity list;
- negotiation or free choice;
- peer instructions, where some children through their previous experience are able to offer others an opening to that learning or context;
- arise spontaneously from an event or interest.

In some circumstances, such as verbal instructions, children almost inevitably appear to believe that we mean everyone else in the room except them, so it is as well to ensure that for this, and other reasons, the children have opportunities to reiterate their perception of the task. This reinforces the requirements for the children and offers teachers an insight into their own communication skills. With younger children, much research (e.g. Tizard and Hughes, 1984; Wells, 1987) has shown that the unfamiliar language of school can inhibit the child's normal communicative competence and performance, and so it is important to allow opportunities for sharing intentions from verbal instructions as often as possible. Peer instruction is particularly useful in this context as children can often communicate easily with each other. The child who has had a period of absence is especially able to benefit from peer guidance, and this can also assist the hard-pressed teacher.

Groups have traditionally been labelled in primary classrooms with colours, animal names or whatever titles appear appropriate at the time or to the topic. Imaginative naming of groups can make useful links with subjects or topics, e.g. groups can be named after famous people, places, buildings, towns within the county area, districts in the town, trees, flowers, forms of transport and so on. Names should not, however, be demeaning to children, have hidden values or be confusing: consider the class groups named after the days of the week and what happened when the Friday group were given their Tuesday tasks!

Classrooms in which a group rotation system is operated, that is where tasks are set in various areas of the classroom and children move around them on a rota basis (timed or according to completion), are normally directed to their tasks by coloured or named pointers moved to denote the class base in which they are to work (see Fig. 4.1).

Allocating activities by task cards is very useful because it does not require the teacher to be in constant verbal communication with large groups of children. It does require a certain reading ability on the part of the children and, of course, preparation by the teacher. However, once made, the cards can be used for different groups. Open written instructions like 'Use the tape-recorder to read your story for other children to listen to' or 'Find out how many times you can write your name before the 3 minute sand timer runs out' could be used over and over again. Such a card can also list the materials required so that children can collect these themselves, for example, 'To make a . . . . . . You will need . . . . . . This is what to do . . . . . .' Pictorial clues may be given for younger or less able children. It is also worth considering use of the computer

*Figure 4.1*  Children in rotating activity situations often have their tasks directed through pointers on a chart

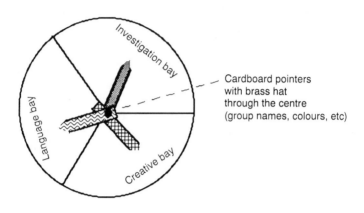

Cardboard pointers with brass hat through the centre (group names, colours, etc)

Class of 30 children rotating around the 3 areas

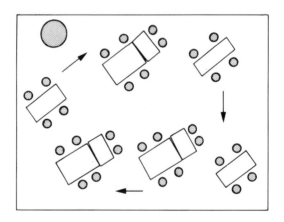

Key:

= teacher          = child

*It is worth considering the use of the computer or tape-recorder for giving instructions to a group.*

or tape-recorder for giving instructions to a group, but teachers should ensure that they try out the procedures at the time of devising the task so as to ensure that all managerial aspects ('Put the tape-recorder on ...... Pause *before* going off to find your materials') have been covered. Computers are now well-used in many classrooms as a resource but still lack use as a teaching tool. Reporting back could also be done via the same media.

Certainly a system which requires children to be part of the planning process for an activity, however minimally, to undertake that activity and complete it and to report back on achievement and progress ensures a satisfactory cycle of learning for children and teacher and should be incorporated as often as possible to ensure children's complete involvement in their tasks. Feedback has been found by many researchers to be the key to both effective teaching and learning.

There are many potential ways in which groupings can occur, but teachers should keep in mind the purposes for the grouping, the practical and physical constraints and advantages of moving the children around in this way, resource provision and whether the processes are beneficial in ensuring timetable demands are met. Whether to use group, class or individual activities is another matter.

## Individual, whole class and group organization and learning

Individualized programmes, such as those used in many mathematics and English schemes, create considerable dilemmas for teachers. First, it is questionable whether they are capable in themselves of generating actual learning; or, as many of the manuals rightly suggest, useful only for check-up purposes. Secondly, as much because of differing task completion speeds as different learning speeds, children will inevitably all be on a different page, though possibly covering very similar material and, therefore, over a short period of time teachers can find themselves repeating the same learning points or instructions over and over again. It is far more efficient and less tedious if children are grouped according to particular concepts covered within the scheme or work books, the teacher then anticipating the next focus and drawing together a group of children working towards that aspect. This will enable teachers to assess efficiently each group's current and future needs, to use teaching time better and allow children the opportunity to share ideas with each other about the learning task. It is far more likely in this situation that teachers will be able to explain intentions and account for different styles than in an exhausting individualized system. This is not denying that there will be one or two children who have quite specific individual needs, but their needs are more likely to be catered for if group learning and teaching has been established for the majority and the teacher is not continually forced to deal with queues of individuals. The latter can only create a reactive teaching situation, whereas the former, with its greater structure, has more proactive potential.

Whether to use whole class, group or individual teaching methods will depend on the curriculum aspect to be covered as well as learning and teaching styles. Using a combination of methods will ensure variety for everyone. It is clearly advantageous to introduce new techniques to all the children, but if the equipment is small or of limited quantity, this may best be done in groups, otherwise not all children will see or be able to handle necessary materials. Using something like music as an inspiration for writing or movement would be extremely difficult to manage for one group as, without a headphone system, the sound would be disruptive to others and, therefore, is appropriately reserved for a quiet whole class time. Using a picture as a stimulus would clearly be more appropriate for group activities, otherwise detail, for example, would be inaccessible to some.

## Whole class methods

What do we mean by whole class teaching and learning and are there different styles? Class teaching can take the form of:

- exposition,
- demonstration,
- discussion,
- shared experience (story, poem, drama, P.E., class visit),
- question and answer sessions,
- problem-solving sessions (could be about something of mutual interest, e.g. classroom rules!),
- rote learning experience (unison poetry reading, reciting tables).

It shares these characteristics with group teaching, which differs mainly in the fact that the rest of the class has also to have their needs met by the teacher at the same time! Therefore, anything which needs to be said to the whole class is probably better conveyed by this means, reinforced by group or individual communication as necessary.

A main mode is undoubtedly that of exposition – the teacher telling or explaining and the children listening. Other methods, such as teacher demonstration, could require individual children contributing verbally or physically (handling materials used) to the proceedings. Participation in its many forms is a requirement of most other whole class methods. While all class teaching strategies can be very useful tools in introducing concepts and practising skills, in order to focus every individual child's attention with maximum efficiency, the teacher's own style and orchestration of whole class sessions needs careful planning and management. Teachers need to experiment to discover which seating and organizational arrangements offer children most opportunity to focus on the teacher. As an example, Neill (1991: 114) suggests from his research that those children facing the teacher make a greater contribution that those sitting sideways, while Wheldall and Glynn (1989) discovered that seating children in rows increased the amount of on-task behaviour, produced better quality work and elicited more praise from the teachers. The authors also claimed that periodically changing children's seating arrangements is also a potent way of influencing classroom operations, thus leaving the way open for variety – though this, of course, could create its own disruptions either physically or because the children's general routines are temporarily disturbed.

In Chapter 1, it was emphasized that a dynamic personality and highly animated way of teaching were found to be two of the characteristics of effective teachers and this applies nowhere more so than in expository or demonstrational teaching. Think what teachers are competing with in the outside world – colour television, video presentations, computers, interactive video facilities, dramatic shop window displays, sophisticated marketing, and so on – to realize the kind of strategies needed to focus and sustain children's attention. Thus personal performance and competency have also to be supported by technical competence in organizing and managing relevant materials. Whole class sessions will include combinations of:

- creating a sense of anticipation in the children about the session;
- varying voice levels and tone;
- looking interesting and interested (physical appearance makes its own statement);
- pacing the session so that it finishes on a rounded note but with a sense of somewhere still to go (not a sense of having 'done' the Romans, but that there is still a lot to learn!);
- well-paced verbal explanations interspersed with visual materials;
- specific eye contact with as many individual children as possible;
- empathy with general 'mood' of class and changing tactics if they become restless or inattentive;
- pitching teaching at a relevant comprehension level for learners;
- physical movement of the teacher;
- elements of surprise, such as taking items out of boxes (guessing games keep most children alert);
- elements of humour (absolutely *not* patronizing, sarcastic or belittling!);
- materials all to hand (nothing turns an audience off more than the teacher having to go in search of a vital piece of equipment);
- making immediate judgements on likely interference and alerting the potential disruptive child to your sensitivity;

- using a variety of technical aids, (e.g. overhead projector, video, computer) to support teaching and keep learners alert.

Although disconcerting, analyzing and evaluating a video of your own classroom teaching is a very worthwhile learning experience. Children can also gain by seeing their own behaviour on tape!

There is no doubt that teaching the whole class at once can be very time-efficient for the teacher and may well be equally effective for the children as part of an overall diverse framework of activities. As we have seen, children have very different styles of learning (as teachers do of teaching) and, if whole class teaching is undertaken, it must acknowledge these different styles. Children who learn effectively through auditory strategies are undoubtedly likely to be at an advantage in exposition to those whose learning is more kinaesthetically orientated. Visual learners may cope with whole class teaching provided that such animation and visual stimulation already discussed are present.

## Grouping for learning

Teaching the whole class is often used as a pre-emptor for group learning, a specific focus being discussed and outlined by the teacher before children are set tasks to make their own investigations, the teacher's time then being spent profitably in communicating with groups and individuals as the need arises. Such groupings may be constructed in various ways for many purposes, the process being highly compatible with the notions of interactionism and constructivism outlined in the previous chapter. Similarly, different styles of learning can be catered for in groups with, for example, innovative learners working with common-sense learners to provide both with a challenge though in different ways.

Many primary teachers regularly group by friendship, ability or mixed ability, though research suggests that these are rarely more than seating arrangements (Galton and Williamson, 1992). Groupings can and should also be made to foster collaborative and cooperative learning settings, promote children's language interactions and for peer tutoring purposes, each of which has received much attention from researchers (e.g. Bennett and Cass, 1988; Topping, 1988; Crouse and Davey, 1989) and are discussed below.

In earlier chapters, the need for keeping the number of main groups as few as possible, was outlined which, as later examined, is not always compatible with notions of group size. Like whole class teaching, group teaching will be undertaken to serve different learning needs in relation to the children and the curriculum. For example, single-sex groupings have been suggested as most likely to enable the development of particular skills in girls, such as technological ability, and counteract boys' perceptions of girls' inabilities in this area (D'Arcy, 1990: 83).

In addition to *ability*, *mixed-ability* and *friendship* arrangements, groups can be allocated on the basis of:

- children's personality (e.g. gregarious/quiet, passive/active, leaders/ followers, highly motivated/less motivated, articulate/less articulate, and so on – see comment in previous chapter);
- age groupings, particularly in vertically grouped classes;
- deliberate mixed-age groups;
- single-sex groups – boys or girls;
- deliberate mixed-sex groups, e.g. Wheldall and Olds (1987) found that time on-task in mixed-sex groups constituted 90 per cent of the session, whereas it was 75 per cent or less in single-sex groups;
- jigsaw groupings, where pairs of children work together and are then joined by another pair (Johnson and Johnson, 1975);
- learning styles (single or intermixed);
- teaching style intended, e.g. those children for whom the next step is to follow a teacher demonstration or learn through modelling;
- for certain circumstances, e.g. religious teaching, different ethnic groupings may be constituted;
- deliberate mixed-race groups.

The diversity of the groupings is matched only by the diversity of the tasks which may be given and many groupings are interchangeable. Group activities could include:

1 All groups doing the same subject and the same focus, e.g. science, either collaboratively or individually.
2 All groups doing the same subject and same focus but at different levels.
3 All groups working on the same subject focus but different tasks, e.g. investigating electricity but doing so through a range of different parallel activities which may then be rotated.
4 Individual groups may have their own focus according to level or interest or be joint-outcome groups where each child's partial contribution is eventually constructed in a whole, e.g. when children have worked independently on aspects of art work which eventually results in a combined product.

5 Teaching groups composed of those children with whom the teacher wishes to work intensively for a period of time.

6 All groups may work on different subjects, or half the groups on English and half on science (if three groups, two could be English and one science). Again groups can be rotated or moved around.

7 Peer-tutored groups, either tutored from within the class or from other classes, perhaps older children helping younger ones.

8 All groups may be given free choice of activities.

9 Spontaneous groupings may form from an interest which has been generated.

If three large groups are the usual way of organizing the children, these groups could also be subdivided on any of these bases. All combinations are useful for different purposes related to the curriculum and intentions for learning, and teachers should be aware of what each has to offer to maximize efficient and effective teaching and learning.

Where ability groups are formed, these must be flexible and continually reformed when covering various aspects of the curriculum, as it is unlikely that children will be equally capable in all areas, perhaps excelling in maths yet struggling with written work. There is some real danger in ability groups, in that children only too readily identify with either end of the spectrum and label themselves and each other. It is possible that teachers, albeit unwittingly, also emphasize abilities, with the 'Rabbits' or 'Yellow group' clearly understanding that they are the 'poor ones' or the 'top group'. It is best to avoid any situations where children's 'academic' standing is made obvious to others, as this can affect self-image on both sides (see Burns, 1982). By forming and re-forming ability groups for curriculum and social purposes, many of these problems can be overcome, but it requires certain broad organizational skills of the teacher which entail:

- identifying the teaching and learning needed in each curriculum area at the various stages;
- identifying where each child is in relation to each curriculum aspect;
- arranging a number of suitable activities for each level in each subject requiring different degrees of teacher involvement;
- allocating the tasks at different levels verbally or on lists;
- being prepared to change these lists as differing progress occurs.

Having explored some of the basic organizational factors under-lying grouping, it is worth dwelling on some aspects further, part-icularly the concept of collaborative group learning, which is felt by many practitioners and researchers to offer a solution to the problem of one teacher constantly dealing with many children.

## Collaborative and cooperative grouping

Collaborative grouping is normally applied to those groups where a collaborative outcome is required, whereas cooperative grouping is undertaken where children work together but produce inde-pendent outcomes (Galton and Williamson, 1992). As Greenfield (1984: 137) suggests, schools have traditionally valued independ-ent rather than cooperative learning and many, therefore, have little experience in implementing the latter. Because of the poten-tial for competition, Casanova (1989: 12) suggests that it is nec-essary to explain to children that they are required to help one another and teachers should emphasize that children are not sharing 'answers' but understanding. While a little competition is useful in prompting children to practise skills and learn through games, it has no real place in collaborative learning situations which em-phasize interacting with each other to everyone's advantage.

Very many studies report children's positive enthusiasm and increased learning opportunities within group situations. Davey (1983: 183), in a study of multi-racial classrooms, found that 'under cooperative group learning conditions, helping behaviour increased, the children felt more liked, more accepted and more concerned about each other . . . many reported themselves as feel-ing better able to cope with their work'. In their study of 11- and 12-year-olds, Bennett and Cass (1988: 31) found that in mixed groups, on-task behaviour was very high and instructional talk was substantially greater than procedural talk. HMI found the best mathematics activities were those in which pupils sought solutions together (DES, 1989) and Dunne and Bennett (1990: 12) found task-related talk increased significantly in cooperative groups of primary children. Hull (1990: 63) asserts that small group games provide excellent contexts for increasing the attention span of some children and allowing them to learn through others' at-tempts. Silveira and Trafford (1988) suggest that those children exhibiting individual needs in school benefit greatly in terms of self-esteem by involvement in group cooperative activities, recog-nizing their similarities with others rather than differences.

Rose (1983: 57) suggests that children find a group setting more attractive than individual work; group learning makes better use of teacher time; the group provides models and feedback from peers; and the group provides opportunities for children to teach others. Group work potentially offers greater opportunity for children to gain metacognitive understanding: in learning about others' learning, children will inevitably learn something about their own.

In the USA, both Slavin (1983) and Johnson and Johnson (1975) found in cooperative learning contexts children's attainment increased, self-esteem was heightened and more positive relationships were formed between pupils irrespective of sex, race or handicap. Galton and Williamson (1992) have made similar findings in the UK.

To implement collaborate group work, first there is a need to consider four factors: the group task, the group composition, the group number and the group seating arrangement. The goal must be clear and appropriate and be achievable rather than open-ended (the latter tasks often providing dissension rather than concordance). The composition of the group depends upon the purposes of the task, but friendship groups may offer the best starting point. Giving each member a definite role to play can modify the impact of dominant personalities (SEAC, *c.* 1990). Once children are really familiar with group work strategies, the composition of the group can be varied but essential collaborative characteristics are retained. Jigsaw groups in particular offer potential here, with two joining two, as the optimum group for primary children appears to be four (Bentley and Rowe, 1991). The seating arrangements must enable children to see and hear each other and resources should be readily available to hand to prevent disruption of discussion in the retrieval of materials. Children's early attempts at collaborative working may be tentative and, as Biott (1984: 10) suggests, it is 'easy to be put off at first by untidy talk that seems to be getting nowhere'. He discovered that 'group work is made up of a series of phases characterized by variations in direction, in depth and in degrees of commitment or intensity' (p. 11). Teachers should also be wary of 'teacherly' intervention, as this removes one important aspect of group work, that of group autonomy. Similarly, any necessary praise or reprimand should also be group directed. Those wishing to study collaborative group work in more detail should consult either Galton and Williamson (1992), or Dunne and Bennett (1990) for theoretical and practical guidance.

The message in all research is that teachers must be prepared to *teach* children to be cooperative and reinforce appropriate skills of cooperation and collaboration through sensitive and positive feedback which does not undermine the group identity, empathy or autonomy. A wealth of useful group identity games outlined in Masheder (1986) and Silveira and Trafford (1988) include many practical group cohesion activities to be undertaken with children.

### Individual teaching and learning

Individual teaching is vital when a specific child has needs very different from the norm, but is only capable of being implemented if the rest of the classroom structures are both geared for it and permit teachers time to operate individualization, which is debatable with classes of 30 or more pupils. It certainly becomes more possible if children are encouraged to work together to solve problems and attempt solutions to questions which arise. The balance between individual activity and group/class activities also needs consideration in the school context, which is, after all, a social setting and intended as a socialization process. All children, including the very able and the less able, may need individual learning opportunities, but most children enjoy working with peers, if only in a pair.

As pointed out by many writers and teachers, a majority of individual needs in the classroom centre around children whose behaviour is inappropriate to the needs of the majority and teachers often have to build a very special individual relationship with these children while emphasizing and acknowledging that their needs often lie as much in social learning as in the intellectual domain. The individual needs of handicapped children are also a vital consideration for the classroom environment if these children are genuinely to have equal opportunities (under The Children Act, 1989) within the normal school (Whitfield, 1991).

Individual learning needs may be met in terms of specific programmes for a particular child, where the teacher sets tasks of a very particular nature or level in an attempt to meet a child's needs. These should require the child to work with others at times and to concentrate alone for short periods (many slower learning children have very short concentration spans). Very able learners who progress quickly through progressive tasks, may also benefit by having specific tasks allocated to them, particularly those which require lateral thinking (Fisher, 1990), in order that they are constantly challenged to think around problems and solutions and do not become bored or turn their talents to less appropriate activities!

In peer-tutoring situations, having to explain something clearly for others to follow can provide a suitable challenge for able children as it helps them order and clarify their own thoughts. This applies equally to less able children who may gain significantly in confidence, knowledge and skills by 'tutoring' another child. As an example, a particularly able child in one of my classes (Kathy) quickly gained quite extensive knowledge of probability and revelled in tutoring another quite able child (Des) whose behaviour had been causing problems. The relationship which grew between them through the peer-tutoring was beneficial in many ways as Kathy, constantly questioned by Des, drove herself to acquiring more and more information to pass on to him and he, in turn, became more responsive to both learning and appropriate behaviour demands, so as to continue being able to work with Kathy.

Similarly, Gary (a slow learning child) developed a relationship with Elaine (a child who was frequently absent from school), and in working with Elaine to ensure that she covered those things missed during absence, Gary was able to reinforce and assimilate his own learning, gain empathy with another learner's needs and, even more importantly, feel a sense of pride in what he had learned. Clearly, these kinds of strategies will need careful monitoring by teachers and will by no means work with all children. Equally, such strategies should not be overused. However, even saving a few minutes in having to explain to an absent child what they have missed, could mean a significant difference for a class teacher in being able to continue the planned teaching and learning (Goodlad, 1979).

This is, of course, by no means the only way of dealing with individual needs or for providing peer-tutoring opportunities. As with any innovation, a teacher embarking upon the process must give it time and start in a very small way with only one or two pairs of children, *both* of whose learning needs may be met within a peer-tutored situation. Peer-tutoring in reading is one area where much positive research has been undertaken (see, e.g. Topping, 1987) and is often a good area in which to begin the process, though any area where specific knowledge and skills are transmitted has been shown to be more successful in terms of quality learning outcomes, for both tutor and tutee (Fitz-Gibbon, 1988). Like collaborative grouping, it also works most effectively if the children have set parameters of goal achievement from the outset rather than open-ended tasks.

ACTIVITY 9

*Consider for a moment*:

- How do you deal with individual needs in the classroom?
- Do you try to do all the additional work with the children yourself?
- Would some form of peer-tutoring help you and the children in your class?
- Can you think of any individuals who would make good tutors?
- Are there any children who would benefit by pairing up to help each other?
- How will the tasks be allocated?
- How can children be guided in appropriate strategies?
- How will they be expected to report back?
- How can you monitor the learning of both children in a peer-tutoring set-up?

In terms of individualized learning programmes, teachers must establish whether a particular child's needs are best met by direct guidance to particular activities decided or designed for that child. Some teachers prefer to operate an individualized system for all children, which is likely to involve having lists of specific activities that can be undertaken by the children in any order during the whole day or part of it and may encourage children to work at their own pace on activities of their choosing according to interest. If children are genuinely working individually on some aspect of learning and developing confidence and independence, this presents no problem, but in some circumstances it can be questionable whether the individuals are doing anything more than occupying their time. Being able to complete a task does not mean you have to understand what you did or why you did it. Misunderstandings may well become clearer and less threatening in a peer group and autonomy is as much the province of a group of children as it is of individuals. Even talking to two children at a time can cut the contact time with the whole class individually by half. To be successful in terms of children's learning, individualized programmes require the teacher to organize 'conference' times, i.e. set certain times aside in the day to discuss with children what they are doing, going to do and hope to achieve within a given time span, and creating other times to give and receive feedback on completed activities.

Whatever the circumstance, class, group or individual, teachers will need to be vigilant in ensuring that children's tasks are purposeful and that learning is carefully monitored, features we will review further in successive chapters. Before moving on, try activity 10.

---

ACTIVITY 10

Having read the above exploration of whole class, group and individual teaching and learning strategies, examine the following list of primary curriculum activities. *What is the most appropriate way of organizing each activity?* (You may qualify or determine other factors within your own classroom as necessary.)

1  Story
2  Shape in maths
3  Science demonstration
4  Clay/woodwork session
5  Spelling tasks
6  Examining an historical artefact
7  Home corner play
8  P.E./movement session
9  Design technology activity
10  Floating and sinking experiment
11  Making a maths game
12  Working on citizenship issues
13  Listening to reading
14  Sex education session

Having made your choice, justify it by responding to the following questions:

- Why is this the most appropriate organization?
- What are the alternatives?
- Will you be able to assess learning in this context?
- How would you explain your decision to the children? colleagues? parent? curriculum adviser? governor?

---

**Equal opportunities**

All children, irrespective of age, race, sex, class, personality or ability, deserve provision of the best possible opportunities for learning within the 'entitlement' curriculum. In the classroom, this sometimes means engineering situations to ensure reality matches rhetoric. It also means understanding something of the issues which underlie equal opportunities which are now well documented and can be only briefly noted herein. Meeting the needs of individuals from all backgrounds and both sexes and providing anti-racist, anti-sexist education are two main strands to be developed in any equal opportunities thinking and action.

Huston and Carpenter (1985: 163) point out significant differences in the learning styles of girls and boys, highlighting such issues as girls more often selecting and thriving in highly structured activities, whereas boys' preference is for a lower structure, factors supported by Solomon and Kendall (1979). Moir and Jessel (1989: 185) suggest that girls' greater bias towards personal and collective situations, means that they should be encouraged to investigate the structure and functioning of mechanical and technical objects in groups rather than individually, which is consistent with the views expressed earlier about group learning. Lockheed (1985: 182) found that cross-sex groupings were instigated by 9- and 10-year-old American children, despite their stated preferences being for single-sex groups. D'Arcy (1990) deliberately set out through small, single-sex group work at the outset, to involve girls in building with constructional toys and, once they were confident enough to hold their own, constituted groups of two girls and two boys and set collaborative activities which proved to offer equality to both sexes.

Teachers should ensure that differential behaviour control techniques, which many researchers have found, are identified and combated: as Eccles and Blumenfeld (1985: 110) suggest, 'being in a classroom in which praise [and criticism] is used differently for boys and girls has a detrimental effect on all girls but not on boys'. In Brophy's (1985: 129) research, it was found that criticism of girls' work by teachers 'almost always indicated that they lacked competence or did not understand the work, whereas criticism of boys' work often referred to non-intellectual aspects that did not imply a lack of competence'. French (1986: 406) found that teachers readily respond to their pupils' inputs and, therefore, as most inputs in whole class time were made by boys, boys received significantly more response time and teacher attention than did girls.

Tape-recording a few interactions with children in group and individual situations would soon alert the teacher to whether this applies in his or her situation. Overt sexism such as that reported by Campbell and Brooker (1990) in a class of 10- to 11-year-olds must be tackled directly, as must expressed racism (Davey, 1983). Sharan (1980: 270) warns that: 'Whatever the emphasis on orientation of the multi-cultural programme adopted by the school, it is unlikely to have a great deal of influence on peer relationships unless what is taught is in harmony with how it is taught.'

This is particularly so in the light of what has been suggested in the previous chapter regarding interactionist/constructivist views of children's learning. Denscombe (1983: 187) found an expressed inconsistency within the children themselves, with many stating that they had friends from other ethnic groups but finding, in field observations, that patterns of pupil interaction did not correspond to expressed friendship choices. Davey (1983: 143) found that teachers were an 'important source of influence in promoting inter-group acceptance' because all children in his study exhibited less in-group bias in the classroom than in other contexts beyond the teacher's control.

Domination of particular activities by particular groups, including playground space, needs to be consistently opposed by both the teacher and the children whom it affects, by discussion, drama and different types of opportunities given through various forms of grouping. Stimulus areas (see Moyles, 1989) can be set up which reflect both different racial groups and appeal to cross-sex groups, e.g. museums, hospitals, a recording studio, a bookshop or a citizens' advice bureau.

Clearly, teachers need continually to evaluate and analyse the situation in their own classes for, although few teachers now still line children up in rows of boys and girls or ask for strong boys to move equipment, there is still a long way to go in ensuring all stereotyping and implicit value statements are finally eradicated.

### Behavioural issues

Without making light of behavioural and control aspects, if the issues already explored in this and previous chapters are fully addressed, teachers will have gone a long way towards ensuring appropriate behaviour is the accepted norm. As the Elton Report (DES, 1989: 12) concluded: 'We conclude that the central problem of disruption could be significantly reduced by helping teachers to become more effective classroom managers.'

This is the one area in particular where individualization is often the key to success, for if the teacher knows each child and the child feels valued by the teacher, then even within group and class settings the teacher can acknowledge understanding of the child's needs. Certainly in the middle and later years of primary schooling, children very much resent being treated differently and the balance here is between ensuring that all the pupils in the class know the boundaries of appropriate behaviour, yet dealing with misdemeanours on an individual counselling basis. It is unlikely ever to be beneficial to either teacher or child to have open confrontation about an issue. Children 'cover up' what their needs really are (as do teachers) for fear of being made to look foolish (Patel, 1991: 3):

> The fear of ridicule governs us all and humour can be the greatest friend or worst enemy. . . . The power of ridicule and humour is still very much alive and well after a long and honourable history.

Inappropriate behaviour such as fighting, shouting out, swearing, sulking, refusing to do something or generally being disruptive is, on the whole, construed through adult values and we often apply adult values to dealing with it: we get very cross and angry when a child has hit or threatened another child, failing often to see, particularly with young children, that this is their way of trying out and understanding relationships and the responses of others. This is not to say that inappropriate behaviour is excusable, but rather that *it is the behaviour which is unacceptable – NOT the child*.

Whatever else, we should not undermine children's confidence in themselves and with it their self-esteem. It is necessary at times to legitimize aggressive or power behaviour and this can be achieved in several ways through activities such as drama and role play and materials such as clay and woodwork, which offer children outlets for physical behaviour, the former also offering a forum for dealing with emotions and relationships. Similarly, formation of certain groups as indicated above can foster different characteristics. Merrett and Wheldall (1990) suggest that teachers need to concentrate on what they can change in children behaving inappropriately rather than what they cannot, particularly home circumstances, a point also taken up by Docking (1990) in his excellent book on managing behaviour.

Forestalling potential areas of dispute by familiarizing oneself with the antecedents of unwanted behaviour and steering the children in another direction is a skill worth developing and grows with experience. However, much unacceptable behaviour occurs because children are uncertain of what they are doing, cannot find the materials needed, have to wait lengthy periods of time for others to respond as the teacher wishes, are bored with work which is unvaried or have few opportunities to work collaboratively with other children. Even something very simple like having a subsidiary activity available for when children have finished a main task can be highly advantageous in ensuring that children's spare moments are not filled with something more unacceptable! As Goodlad (1983: 556) believes: 'If academic learning does not engage students, something else will.' Teaching and training have a significant bearing here: how can children know what is appropriate behaviour in any particular classroom unless this is discussed with them and children are taught the necessary skills? Bull and Solity (1987: 17) make a very worthwhile point:

> when planning our teaching of new educational skills our first concern is the management of setting events for the children's behaviour. . . . This idea of setting up the situation so as to help pupils respond with appropriate behaviour from the outset is perhaps less familiar.

This again raises the point of sharing with children what they are doing and why they are doing it and adds the dimension of how they should set about the task, with whom and in what ways.

Teachers also need to be encouraged not to jump to conclusions. The 'count to 10' rule before intervening is a most useful strategy in that it allows the teacher time to note what is actually taking place and, therefore, make a more appropriate assessment of the situation. Calderhead (1984: 60) suggests that teachers, for example, generally respond to inattention with a motivating or disciplinary response, whereas often the inappropriate behaviour may be the outcome of the child experiencing a learning difficulty.

The former often compounds and reinforces the teacher's expectations of the child and thus generates a self-fulfilling prophecy. Good and Brophy (1984: 11) offer the suggestion that 'by implying that it was expected, the teacher subtly condoned misbehaviour and made it more likely'.

The messages in much research are clear: a well-organized classroom can go a long way to ensuring that appropriate behaviour is present at most times. When the system breaks down for any reason, deal with the unwanted behaviour as a classroom issue, at the same time identifying children who may need particular guidance or counselling. Summarizing the results of personal experience and reading, the issues appear to be:

- Organize with an anticipation of appropriate behaviour and manage any unwanted behaviour by identifying antecedents and changing strategies accordingly.
- Avoid confrontation with children at all costs, particularly in making generalizations about class behaviour or home circumstances.
- Be honest with children about your own feelings on the issue of the types of inappropriate behaviour which have an adverse affect on everyone.
- Create a collaborative working environment among the children, involving them in decisions about classroom rules and procedures (Docking, 1990).
- Maintain a sense of humour and try to understand the child's point of view in a conflict situation rather than applying adult values.
- Be fair and consistent at all times with all children, listen to explanations (very difficult!) and blame the behaviour, not the child personally.
- Praise that which is really praiseworthy (the act not necessarily the child: see Holt, 1991) and express genuine concern when appropriate.
- Dwell on the positive rather than the negative, reinforcing the most appropriate behaviour through positive comment rather than communicating with class, group and individuals only when something is wrong.
- Undertake group dynamic activities, such as parachute games, in order to create a class social identity.
- Offer a quiet, cooling off time in a comfortable spot within sight of the teacher to any child who has been reprimanded for inappropriate behaviour. Find something pleasant to discuss with the child when appropriate behaviour is re-established.
- Accept and acknowledge support from others for those children for whom even the best strategies do not work – for the sake of yourself and the class as a whole.

## Conclusion

It is quite remarkable how good teachers are able to establish such a complexity of rules and working conventions, often with quite young children, sometimes with children from a very unruly background, without appearing to nag all the time, or be rigid or dictatorial (Wragg, 1991: 4).

Ensuring all children understand the classroom learning context and have respect for the teacher, each other and the physical environment means sharing all its 'secrets', training children in a variety of skills and trusting them. Through these strategies, satisfactory relationships are, at the very least, afforded a chance of developing. Reminding children periodically of the reasons for rules and routines and being flexible when necessary, ensures smooth management. The balance required is in teachers providing for every child's learning at an intellectual and social level within a variety of situations, yet at the same time encouraging children to learn from each other and respect each other's differences. Bull and Solity (1987: 29) suggest:

> If the teacher is to enable children to make sense of their environment, to learn new behaviours readily and to maintain them, it is crucial that his [*sic*] classroom management is consistent from day to day and from week to week.

Consistency is, as indicated above, to do with planning – 'to fail to plan is the plan to fail' (Pernet, 1989: 7). Crucial to planning are factors of timetabling and the general management of time, the subject of Chapter 5.

# 5

## Time for teaching
## and learning

Whether to organise for whole class teaching and learning, for
group or individual activities is highly dependent upon the classroom and school context, the children, the learning intentions, the
individual teacher's style and approach and, above all, time factors. An attempt to cover the entire legislated curriculum with
each individual child in the time allotted within the normal working day is bound to fail and leave teachers feeling somewhat less
than enthusiastic and proactive. Time, as the modern world per-
ceives it, is finite, particularly the school day. What to leave out
becomes more important than what to retain. In relation to the
notion of balance, which has pervaded previous chapters, the concept of time is incompatible, for it rarely balances adequately with
what we want to achieve. For primary teachers, their work may
be pursued long hours into non-directed time (Campbell *et al.*,
1991) – and it is a mark of their professionalism and concern for
children that so many of them have been prepared to sustain this
without antagonism in an attempt to meet unprecedented legislative
demands.

Now that the main curriculum requirements are known, it is
perhaps the right moment to think proactively about the question
of the time needed to fit everything in, for as suggested by Ball
*et al.* (1984: 57):

> ... empirically, conceptually and theoretically, time has been
> virtually ignored by sociologists of education as a phenomenal

aspect of school. And yet it is a fundamental organizing principle of the everyday life world of schooling; it penetrates deeply into the organizational and curricular experiences of the pupil and of the teacher and is a crucial factor in the shaping and ordering of the curriculum in action at every level.

A dilemma for teachers is that the new demands on the precious resource of time mean that considerable spontaneity has gone from the role of teaching and everything must now be far more precise and more curriculum, rather than child, orientated – at least in the planning stages. The shift of emphasis is now certainly on teachers to predict from the appropriate stages in the curriculum guidelines how children can be encouraged to *want* to do what the teacher knows they *must* do in the time available to do it (Wood, 1991: 114). Under the present climate, the role of teacher has reached new dimensions which as yet have been barely internalized. What the public at large and parents in particular can have confidence in, is that teachers are well up to the challenge. Rethinking aspects of their role will be refreshing to many teachers and add new insights into their relationships with children and their ability to promote learning.

Other dilemmas centre around philosophy: if we believe that children cannot learn without constant, direct teaching, then inevitably, with one teacher to 30 plus children, time problems exist. If we believe children can learn without teaching, we are denigrating our own roles! An ongoing dilemma is raised by Alexander *et al.* (1989: 283–4):

> ... the more accessible teachers seek to make themselves to all their pupils as individuals, the less time they have for direct, extended and challenging interactions with any of them; but the more time they give to such extended interaction with *some* children, the less demanding on them as teachers must be the activities they give to the rest; the less demanding of their time and attention as teachers, the more likelihood that the activity in question will demand very little of the child.

A solution perhaps lies in examining the relationship between the aspects of teaching, learning and time and whether anything which is currently done can be jettisoned or redirected in favour of another method or means of achieving the desired outcome (Thody, 1990). The need for time, it must be remembered, is not only the teacher's but the children's. Certain aspects of time in the

*Making appropriate use of all resources can save precious teacher-time.*

day are crucial and relate mainly to how much time is available, how it is spent by whom and whether that use is profitable in terms of children's learning. It is the former to which we now turn, for as (Pernet 1989: 7) suggests: 'In preparing to use our time more effectively, the first things we really need to know are the facts, not the feelings. A record of where our time is really spent is an important first step.'

Richardson (1984: 22) suggests two golden rules regarding time which are worth remembering:

1 You can always make more effective use of time.
2 The only person to make better use of your time is you!

### Time and the timetable

In school it appears that 'The present is always seen to be a matter of progress in relation to time passed and the time remaining measured against these fixed reference points' (Ball *et al.*, 1984: 41) with very little space in between. Working to very tight deadlines at all times can be both useful in focusing the mind but exhausting in generating stress. Time is needed to plan, organize (mostly dealt with in the previous chapters), implement, monitor and evaluate aspects of the classroom situation. As the latter are covered in

Chapter 7, it is the issues of planning and implementing through the timetable and structure of the day which provide the main focus.

## *Planning*

One absolute essential is to plan in detail – time spent in planning is rarely wasted because having a written, internalized plan often frees the mind for dealing with other issues by providing an inherent structure. As Haynes (1987: 39) suggests: 'Planning makes two contributions which bring order to your life. First it tells you how to get from where you are to where you want to be. Second, it identifies the resources required to get you there.'

Classroom and curriculum planning is usually best handled by working from long-term goals and gradually refining them, within the time-scale, to short-term objectives for the week and ultimately the day. Much of the classroom research already included in previous chapters has shown that, of those relatively few primary teachers who did generate plans, most planned in reverse, taking the daily events as the basis and rarely getting into long-term planning. This is, of course, consistent with a child-centred view, in that any plans could be upended in a sudden change of direction desirable for certain individuals. It could also be one of the main reasons why the long-term planning required under the National Curriculum has been so time-consuming and intrusive for some teachers.

Written planning is vital in that it means teachers have a constant source of reference to their long- and short-term intentions and will not waste time in constantly having to remember – and perhaps forgetting. Any changes which are made due to an unexpected or spontaneous response to needs should as quickly as possible be noted on the original plans and concentrated within the time available or, if suitable, replacing something else which is now rendered unnecessary. (Remember it cannot be incorporated as well – only instead!)

Depending on the time available in the day and week, most teachers will want to include periods of whole class teaching, group teaching and individual work and to monitor both contact with individuals and the suitability of features of the learning environment. Sustained daily contact with every child is the ideal rather than the reality and, similarly, it will only be certain times of any week which can be given to monitoring the effectiveness of classroom systems. Some physical contexts (e.g. open-plan bases) mean that teachers must agree to specific periods in the day which will be determined for certain activities in order to minimize noise and maximize effective contact with all the children.

Within the National Curriculum framework, teachers and schools will have made certain decisions as to what a particular year group will be expected to cover by way of subjects and perhaps topics. How these long-term plans are implemented and converted to a teaching and learning framework will depend upon other factors, including:

- the time of year;
- whole school decisions;
- the relative length of each term;
- any 'fixed' aspects, e.g. festivals, celebrations;
- the strengths and expertise of other staff members (to be discussed in Chapter 6);
- the resources available (find out what the school and classroom have to offer and commit it to paper as useful reference material. Better still, make a resource booklet for the whole school – if you have time!). Other services, such as the museum and library, can also help;
- the governors' views on curriculum provision.

Although the individual teacher's way of working is also important, as emphasized in previous chapters, professional development means occasional reappraisal of current practice to incorporate features, such as more whole class teaching, which appear increasingly necessary for implementing full curriculum demands.

Yearly plans normally become termly plans, then half-termly, weekly and daily plans. Schools using a topic approach may offer year groups up to six topics, one for each half-term – with older children this may be as few as three (one for each term). Where schools adopt a more subject approach, particular programmes of study will be identified for year groups, clustered for each subject and then similarly dispersed between terms, half-terms, weeks and days. As each half-term is on average 6–7 weeks, this gives 30–35 days for each topic or set of subject-focused activities to be undertaken. As most timetables in primary schools operate on a weekly basis in terms of fixed days and times for assemblies, playtimes, whole school meetings and so on, it is essential to establish within this week exactly how much time is teacher-children contact time.

## ACTIVITY 11

Use a 5-day grid similar to the following, customized to your week. List all those aspects which are 'fixed' in terms of time needed. Hatch or colour in these aspects to show where control of time is not directly your own.

| day/ time | Monday | Tuesday | Wednesday | Thursday | Friday |
|-----------|--------|---------|-----------|----------|--------|
| 1 hour    |        |         |           |          |        |
| 2 hours   |        |         |           |          |        |
| 3 hours   |        |         |           |          |        |
| 4 hours   |        |         |           |          |        |
| 5 hours   |        |         |           |          |        |

- Do not forget to include a small amount of time which you must have to move children around the school, get coats, toileting, etc. Richardson (1984: 10) suggests that as people mostly underestimate the time needed for tasks, it is necessary to add around 20 per cent to any estimate.
- Include time for the unexpected: this allows elbow room, and when it is not needed gives opportunity for all those little things which are important but seem always to be left. A note on the classroom wall of what these are – go through the five times table with class/group – saves time and mental energy in re-membering.
- Identify, with a different hatching or colour, specific general resource provision – hall times, computer times and so on, which will also be significant in your planning and may be curriculum-specific.

From this activity you should now be able to estimate exactly what time, in what proportions and on what days, is actually available for teaching. Time to establish from the longer and medium term plans what you can actually incorporate in fairly immediate objectives is next. You are now working from what you actually have rather than basing a timetable on wishful thinking! Further decisions need to be made on priorities

- What MUST you include?
- What SHOULD you include?
- What would you LIKE to include?
  (Arnold, 1988: 85)

This is the crux of the matter. It may be that you find you have insufficient time for all of these and clearly what you *must* include has to have priority. (Back to the drawing board in terms of staff and headteacher consultations if you find yourself unable to plot in the 'musts'.) The 'shoulds' have next priority but, because what you and the children may like to do is really important to motivation and interest, try to balance these two elements. Do write down these plans at all stages in a form with which you yourself can work – flow diagrams and webs are used most frequently by teachers, but a time-line is an excellent way of seeing time passing and potential inclusions (see Fig. 5.1).

Plans are needed which incorporate both a view of subject knowledge but also skills and processes to be covered. It is essential that plans show all of these and good examples are given in Leicestershire LEA's *Keystages* document (LCC, 1989). The proportion of time distributed to each subject will basically have been included in the long-term planning but, for primary teachers, the question of gaining sufficient time for basic skills teaching and learning has prominence.

### Basic skills and the curriculum

Lower primary teachers in particular feel strongly that the basic skills of maths, English and science are important because they are core/basic skills and some difficulties have been experienced in covering these within present planning *and* incorporating other curriculum aspects. However, simply by being basic skills they are *always* an integral part of other curriculum aspects, basic to everything we do in our lives. Time can be created by recognizing the core component in foundation curriculum work, and emphasizing it to oneself and the children. For example, history absolutely requires speaking and listening, writing and reading stories,

*Figure 5.1* Time lines are an excellent way of seeing time passing and how it is used

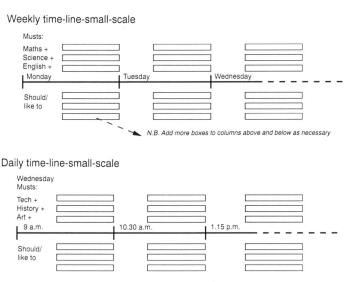

investigating artefacts and drama activities; geography has strong science links; music is related to patterns in mathematics and movement activities. These are much more 'natural' and realistic settings (as far as anything in school is so) than forcing children through a scheme or course book which bears little relevance to the knowledge and skills needed for other learning. The most appropriate learning has always to be that which is understandable, transferable and usable in another context.

Reading is the most fundamental of the basic skills and making time for listening to children read is every primary teacher's major headache. There are few totally satisfactory solutions, but one of these is ensuring that reading is planned for and that those plans are only deviated from in the direst emergency. Identifying the purpose for children's reading helps planning: children can be heard to read in a general way by any helpers in the classroom and this includes other children. However, hearing children read for diagnostic purposes, to find out where they are, whether progress is satisfactory and further teaching required must be the domain of the teacher (be it the class teacher or a peripatetic teacher designated to this task). If this is accepted, the teacher needs to hear older children read for assessment purposes about once a month; with younger children once a week or fortnight should be the aim. Other reading is for pleasure and for practice, to be done as often as possible. Teachers and children should also acknowledge the fact that reading is required in almost every other class activity and does not only relate to a particular 'reading' or story book used by the child. Ensuring children read any written tasks they have done to a friend, other adults, visitors, the whole class or group, would mean most children reading something most days. Provided the class has a matched set of identical books, some reading could also be done in groups with or without the teacher, the children reading a portion of the story or page and then passing on to the next child until all or some of the story is finished. By making requests around the school, it is usually possible to form a set of four to six books and is worth the effort, particularly if the group are roughly matched in terms of oral reading skills. Slower readers should be encouraged to read short books and only attempt one meaningful chunk (a sentence or paragraph) each before passing on to the next child. A helper or more able child might be incorporated into the group with a brief to keep the storyline running smoothly. This should not, of course, be the only reading strategy adopted.

In relation to learning time, it must be acknowledged that there is a difference between allocated and engaged time (Myers, 1990: 13), in that the teacher may plan 30 minutes of English, say 10 minutes exposition and 20 minutes of individual follow-up activity, but the children may take 2–3 minutes to tune-in to the teacher talking and then may actually only be engaged on their own activities for 10 minutes or so because of getting their thinking 'into gear'. Planned teaching time will not necessarily be equivalent to learning time. It is necessary to be realistic about this – and not panic! If all the organizational factors are in place (in other words, children are not wasting time collecting materials, sharpening pencils, finding rubbers and so on) and presented tasks are motivating and interesting, at least maximum engaged time is possible and likely, though individual personalities may still not always put it to best use.

Armed with all these thoughts and written plans, a daily time-table will have emerged which now needs placing in relation to the structure of the day.

### Structuring the day

In order to progress smoothly, both teacher and children need to have a clear view of how each day is basically structured: sharing the class timetable together is one way of doing this. Having a clear, large copy displayed on the class noticeboard enables children to gain a sense of what learning can be anticipated and how much time is available; younger ones will, of course, take longer to gain this understanding and all ages will benefit by some sharing of information with the teacher. Ensuring that they also understand the flow of time in the school day and the various subjects and other aspects which need to be incorporated, gives children a sense of responsibility and ownership over their collective school lives. If children are to be taught to plan and think ahead (Fisher, 1990) and be aware of the vital ingredients of the learning environment, then they must also understand how the day progresses. Sharing this information with one of my own year 3 classes made a very significant difference to the quantity and quality of activities they were able to undertake successfully in any day and week and the individual and group collaborative goal of specific achievement ensured much more focused and engaged time on the children's part.

A school day is 'naturally' broken up into three main sections – before and after play in the morning and the afternoon – though these times are by no means equal. In relation to the kind of classroom organization discussed earlier, however, they give periods of time relevant to children working in particular areas or bays. For younger children, each session can be halved, giving the opportunity for six different foci to the day if necessary. Each of these three or six main sessions will need a firm beginning and rounded ending to ensure that teacher and children feel a sense of achievement, progression and satisfaction.

There is the question of those children who wish or need to sustain a particular activity for a longer period, for example, writing a story or pursuing a science experiment. Predicting the length of achievement time a particular activity will need to achieve a satisfactory outcome, *at least for today* (groups and individuals will, of course, vary in this), is another dilemma. Sometimes pursuing the task that day is vital, but leaving some tasks and coming back to them later may prompt subconscious thinking which can have later beneficial outcomes. It is useful to have a system of 'trade-off' negotiation with children, whereby they are involved in the planning of how they are going to meet daily/weekly 'targets' when unpredicted time is needed for completion of specific activities. Although resisting any commercial and industrial product-centred approach to education, the analogy of the classroom being a mini-company in which the manager collaborates with the

*Some children may wish to sustain a particular activity for a longer period.*

workers to set targets and work schedules, organize appropriate resources, make decisions and then evaluate 'productivity' outcomes (learning), is appealing and consistent with good classroom management.

## Teaching and learning time

The term 'integrated day' is generally interpreted as meaning a daily structure based around different children undertaking different aspects of subject learning at various overlapping times in the day. Although considered, it has come under criticism through potentially lacking the necessary structure deemed to be essential for teaching and learning to be really effective (Mortimore *et al.*, 1988). The obverse is definitely not the disintegrated day! Rather, it is a day structured around specific times for specific tasks, preferably tasks specified by the teacher (for it is she or he who has the overall plan for curriculum coverage) but with some choice for the children (Galton, 1989). The skill of the teacher lies in ensuring that children are motivated by the tasks and take ownership over them, for personal or group ownership goes a long way to ensuring both concentration and quality of outcome.

Bringing the children together at certain times in the day

reinforces the cohesion of the class – this means both physically and mentally, e.g. a story session on the carpet where they all sit together, a drama session or everyone working as a class on a particular subject or theme. For potentially deviant members, classwork provides a forum in which appropriate behaviour can be exemplified and peer pressures can be brought to bear in a fairly obvious way. Kept fairly brief, particularly in the early days with a class, it becomes a positive and well-paced experience for everyone having a definite intention clearly stated by the teacher. If children's involvement is required, tell them so – and vice versa!

Teachers need to decide what they should actually *teach* and what children may learn best by finding out for themselves. Some things, however, are better taught, for example, teaching new art techniques. Having such skills and processes 'up their sleeves' eventually allows children greater personal choice, as they will be able to select a medium appropriate for a specific task.

Some teachers like to structure curriculum time through the use of topics or projects and there are contrasting views on whether this is, or is not, the best teaching and learning framework. Advocates suggest that, among other good reasons, primary children do not think in separate subjects and a holistic way of learning matches primary children's cognitive development. Opponents of topic work suggest that knowledge, skills and understanding are often lost in the wealth of ideas within a topic and can only be covered superficially and, in any case, there are still a range of different subjects to be covered whether we articulate these with the children or not. Both of these are, in their own way, correct, for whether topic or subject, primary children need to have learning established in a context which makes sense and which has relevance to their everyday lives. Science done for the sake of pure experiment is only one aspect of science and unlikely to have immediately transferable knowledge and skills for children, whereas put into the context of cooking and noting changes under heat (and having something to eat at the end), the processes, knowledge and skills gained are far more likely to be remembered.

'Where you do what in the time available is crucial to the success of the what' (Haigh, 1990: 14), and this applies to both timing of activities in the day and over the week, term and year. A wild and windy playtime followed by a very physically active session is likely to be a recipe for chaos. Successive sessions of seated written work are a seedbed for discontentment. This does not mean that always the obverse is needed; for example, if children come in from lunch or playtime with loud voices, 5 minutes of using them to good purpose in singing or reciting a favourite poem will gradually add the necessary voice control.

## Routines

Everyone needs routines in the day, particularly where large groups of people work together, so that they can feel secure enough in the consistency of the setting and its requirements to delve into the less predictable (learning) from a secure base. As Powell and Solity (1990: 81) suggest:

> Routines . . . are the accepted ways of doings things which lend a sense of order and purpose to daily life. The difference between personal routines . . . and collective organizational routines . . . is that the collective routines need agreement, explicitly or implicitly, to work.

Neither routines nor structure need to be fixed and permanent; teachers and children will revel in occasionally doing something different. However, if every day is quite dissimilar and lacking a communicable structure, the best planning in the world will not ensure curriculum coverage and appropriate learning opportunities. Consistency with variety is the order of the day if all teaching and learning styles are to be accommodated. Entwhistle (1988: 242) suggests that 'informal methods which emphasize variety of activities . . . may be valuable for the least able or most autonomous children . . . brighter, highly motivated children appreciate orderliness in the class and structure in the curriculum'.

With routines and structures come *rules* to ensure that all comply with the underlying requirements of the situation. Children *must* be involved in generating and writing those rules if they are to mean anything at all. Pollard (1987: 177) describes this as a 'working consensus' to be negotiated openly with the children. 'Walk in the corridor' or 'Wash your hands before dinner' only have real meaning when one understands the safety concepts which they embrace: children's understanding must be developed from discussion not only about the rules but what underlies them and why they are important to everyone.

Wragg (1991: 4) is right to remind us that 'Learning to understand, follow, sometimes make, and occasionally break rules is an important part of children's personal and social education.' Routines and structure tend to generate rules which need everyone's adherence. Rules prevent things going wrong rather than act as an encouragement towards good behaviour (Cullingford, 1991: 74).

## Match and mismatch

Children's time can be saved by ensuring that the tasks are appropriate to their identified needs. No-one can tell teachers directly how to identify needs because it depends on the particular curriculum aspect to be covered at the time. One move forward is in finding out, as indicated earlier, where children's current knowledge lies. Often we cannot know this, so make a professional 'guess', set up a learning situation and then observe children in their various activities and what they seem able to do. Younger children may have some difficulty in verbalizing their understanding, but skills and processes can both be assessed through observation. Listening to children talking together can give insights into other knowledge. This is where individualization really comes into its own! If the rest of the classroom structures are well established, this necessary observation and listening time will readily follow, whereas the teacher who has to keep reacting to a number of different requests for materials, information or guidance will find this extremely difficult.

## Beginnings and endings

Beginnings and endings of days and sessions are particularly important periods. At the start of the day, there could be many people (parents, school secretary, headteacher) who wish to communicate with the teacher just at a time when he or she really wants to achieve some class cohesion and set up the framework of the day with the children. It is as well to ensure that there is an activity of some kind for children to do at the start of the day – selecting and browsing through books, drawing a weather picture for the day, using odd-shaped paper trimmings and covering them with an appropriate shape pattern, writing sentences to do with currently used words or doing some basic calculations indicated on a board or chart – though it needs to be accepted that these will, on the whole, be 'holding' or practice tasks which do not require teacher input. This process should be explained to the children. 'Can't you see that I'm talking to a parent?' is a crisis or reactive response to a child's interruptions. A more appropriate proactive approach would be to discuss this period of the day with the children as being one in which you may need to speak to others and need an uninterrupted 10 minutes each morning; then insist that they allow you this time. You must then stick to this 10 minutes and not allow it to be regularly extended or children will lose faith and still interrupt.

As with every situation, there are also other alternatives, for example, is this start to the day appropriate for everyone? The younger the children the more likely it is that parents will want to speak to the teacher, but it is certainly possible to set aside certain mornings or afternoons for parent discussions and then to communicate this to parents. A notice in a suitable position *outside* the class area on which parents can select a discussion time is useful, with small matters being communicated in writing, e.g. the doctor's appointment. Emergencies are, of course, as always to be dealt with individually, but a balance needs to be struck between dealing with certain parents who will want to discuss everything with the teacher every day with those who will rarely approach.

In terms of in-school communication, if many of the teachers feel that they have unnecessary interruptions at the start or end of sessions, it is worth raising this as a point for discussion at staff meetings. It could well be that the person doing the interrupting has no idea that this is an inappropriate time.

The register, albeit something of a nuisance, is still a vital document in the school day for fire regulations and knowing who is in attendance should the unthinkable occur. It can be very boring for both teacher and children and ways must be considered to make registration more interesting. When children know the usual name order, a 'silent' register can start the day quietly with children simply following on with saying their names – to make it really difficult, try reverse alphabetical order. Younger children often like to have a picture of themselves which they place in hoops or drawn circles to indicate that they are present and that they are having packed lunches, school dinner or going home. Infants often like to do this with the accompanying parent. Taking one's name off a row of hooks, or revealing a name by lifting off a coloured card, gives children a sense of responsibility and means the teacher can see immediately who is late or absent and can then complete the register while the children work on the first activity. Duplicated class lists near the door (perhaps with five boxes for each day of the week) mean that children can either strike out their names as they arrive or tick a box at the side to say they are present.

It is almost never useful to have highly practical resources and materials readily available to children at the start of the morning, because much time will be needed to clear it away when the main classroom activities are to begin. If materials for the first session are laid on tables, children will need to be trained to ignore them! (I once remember trying to deal with a particularly difficult parent while a group were exploring the tambourines, bells and shakers which were available for the first session on creating sound – needless to say, we all ended up shouting at each other!) If practical materials need to be provided for the first session, they are best stored in tubs or boxes which can be speedily arranged on tables when necessary. However, teachers should aim, as already discussed in Chapter 2, to have the materials available for collection *by the children*, if necessary producing a list of basic materials to be collected by each group.

Another beginning is in relation to a new focus, be it a topic or subject element. Although a basic instinct is to sit children down and talk to them about the new learning, particularly in relation to history and geography, topics may have a more effective beginning through the exploration of an artefact or picture. Such an object could, in time, form the basis of the ending as children could recall and discuss how far they have come in terms of understanding since the first encounter. This is not to deny learning intentions, but these can easily be discussed after the period of exploration which could, in itself, be a type of guessing game. It is often the case that teachers hold up a very small object, say a 5-cm square shape and ask children about its properties: how often this can be seen clearly by every child in the class must be open to conjecture. Were children to explore the shapes first and then gather to discuss them, success in responding could be more predictable.

Friday afternoons, notoriously a 'finishing off' session, might also be put to greater use if at least part of it was given a focus appropriate to the following week. As a teacher, I often discussed with the children on Friday afternoon, through the use of a picture or artefact, something we would be covering the following week and this nearly always prompted some children to bring in materials on Monday which could be used as motivation for others. This gave the children a sense of ownership over the new focus and also provided opportunities for them to share a class interest with parents and think about any knowledge and understanding already existing.

## Changing activities

We all take our own time to accomplish learning and one could say that there are two kinds of time – that which the teacher *allows* and that which the child *needs* (Knight, 1989). However, children (and adults) will ensure that 'work expands to fit the time available' (Parkinson's Law) if all that follows one session of relatively similar or uninteresting work is more of the same! Time limits need to be set for completion of work, variation ensured in subsequent activities through careful planning, and 'time-on-task' monitored.

Although older children can sit for longer periods, variety in the timetable will offer better concentration for all ages. Most days will consist for the children of activities centred around:

● practical activities of various kinds, e.g. experimenting, constructing, making;
● writing and reporting;
● problem solving;
● discussing and listening (with teacher or peers);
● making some choices;
● practising a range of skills.

All these should require the application of existing knowledge and processes. Fairly static activities need interspersing with those which require movement, but this need not be consistent across a class, for example, not everyone should be moving at the same time and may only be seat-based simultaneously for whole class teaching sessions. Advance warning should be given that a change is approaching – there is nothing more annoying and likely to cause disturbance than being told to stop when 2–3 minutes more are needed for satisfactory completion. A 5-minute warning – which is adhered to – starts the process of rounding off the session and hurrying those children who have begun to flag!

Where children change activities within the day, directed or spontaneously, the teacher's management must include ensuring that children understand the need to:

● Complete one task to an appropriate level (and perhaps state of completion) before the next is begun.
● Leave the previous activity area tidy for another person to begin. This may mean putting everything away or moving things to the centre of the table to be drawn on by other children.
● Put their completed task in an appropriate place. A completed task tray is useful for written work and drawings; models will need different provision as emphasized in Chapter 2. Whatever the system, children must know it and respect it.
● Move around the room without disruption to others and respect the fact that other children may not wish to be interrupted.

It is unwise and unhelpful if all children are in the process of changing activities at the same time. If the structure of a particular day requires this, however, the teacher will need to manage the changeover by either permitting only one group at a time to move or by ensuring a smooth rotation at once. On occasions like playtime, allow one group at a time to leave if possible, rather than have a mass exodus, or operate a system whereby children leave alphabetically according to family name, Allens long before Williamses – occasional reverse order will ensure fairness.

## Interruptions

The younger the children the more they appear to need teacher assurance in relation to their tasks and their learning, but sometimes this can just become a habit or be done because the children think (by the way the teacher reacts promptly to every request) that this is the appropriate behaviour to adopt. From the early days in primary school, teachers can make it clear to children that there are many ways of gaining information or assurance without respite to the teacher. Having the materials and resource clearly labelled and available – and pointing this out to the children periodically – can dispense with many unnecessary interruptions. We need to teach children to ask each other or use the classroom as a resource *first* before they ask the teacher and ensure, as suggested in the last chapter, that they are taught to help each other in cooperative or peer-tutored situations. Dunne and Bennett (1990: 32) have shown that this can significantly increase the teacher's own time for essential teaching.

Varley and Busher (1989: 65) researched primary classroom interruptions and found that 'class teachers dealt with over two interruptions per minute for every minute of every day'. Interruption became disruption when it prevented the flow of the activities continuing. To save being interrupted during a story, put a notice on the classroom door to say you do not wish to be disturbed – the children will happily make one. Nothing is more annoying than when the scene is set, the atmosphere is perfect, everyone is interested and then you are interrupted. Perhaps the children can devise a strategy for preventing it happening and try it out themselves – good for encouraging problem solving. Interruptions not only waste useful time but take their toll on emotional energy. Constantly picking up the pieces is stressful, as one always has to work twice as hard to redeem the earlier atmosphere created for the purpose.

*Playtimes*

Many schools have abandoned afternoon playtime because of its brevity. It is worth considering, as an individual teacher and as a staff team, what playtime provides and for whom. Much time after play can be wasted in sorting out playground problems which are outside the individual teacher's knowledge and control. A system which has worked particularly well in some schools is for individual teachers to take their children outside at an appropriate time in the morning when the children (and teacher) appear to need a break (Blatchford, 1989). This event can then also be linked with what is currently in progress in the classroom if wished. In most schools, a 15-minute break is insufficient time for many teachers even to get to the staffroom (which may be located some distance away), and so a mobile tea/coffee facility may prove more satisfactory. Children will still have the opportunity to meet friends from other classes during the lunchtime break – as will teachers.

*Tidy-up time: The teacher's Waterloo!*

All children must tidy up for themselves – not just a willing few – so that they are made aware of the vital ingredients of the learning environment and its needs and, more importantly, their responsibility to others. This can be the most difficult time of the day and new teachers rarely allocate sufficient time. It is always better to allow too much time than too little. A range of practical activities will take at least 15 minutes to tidy away satisfactorily dependent upon the quantity of materials and age of the children. If it happens more quickly, then the time is valuable for discussion, poetry, sharing thoughts on the day, recalling learning outcomes and so on. A useful routine is:

1　Give the children a 5-minute warning coupled with a statement that no new equipment or materials should be sought.
2　At the end of 5 minutes, stop everyone including yourself and get the children to sit down or stand next to where they have been doing tasks.
3　Tell the children that you are going to allocate specific jobs to children to be done after you have completed making the allocations – 'Sally, please collect all the scissors', 'Wayne please put all the paint pots back in the tray' – ensuring that all children serve the needs of the class over a period of time.
4　Tell the child helpers that as soon as they have finished they are to join the rest of the class.

*All children must tidy up for themselves – and be given the appropriate tools and opportunities for doing so.*

5  All those without a task – normally about two-thirds of the class – are instructed to either stay seated and help by putting materials into piles in the centre of the table, or to sit in the carpet area where they can either work with the teacher/other adult, read a book or share experiences from the day, week and term. The children themselves can also be allocated a 'teacher role' occasionally.

Though tasks could be allocated via helper lists, the full procedure is still necessary but instructions at (3) above can be briefer. An alternative, if the classroom size and layout permits, is to ask children to leave the activities and sit in a predetermined place (e.g. the carpet area) and then for the teacher to distribute clearing away tasks from this base, continuing to work with the main class group while the helpers move about their tasks. What the teacher should definitely *not* do is rush around the class tidying up – a supervisory role is the most appropriate on this occasion. An instruction to 'Tidy away now' is definitely for the most experienced and those who have a well-established relationship with the class.

All these systems require an element of 'training', a term on the whole resisted by many. However, one would not expect a football team to learn how to work together effectively to achieve results without an element of training as a basic cooperational skill. Training, after all, is only the means by which certain skills are acquired and, having been acquired, can then make other learning more accessible. So it is with children: we can only expect all the classroom routines and structures to operate efficiently if the children have received training and teaching in what, how and why.

## Gaining more time in small ways

Primary teachers are frequently (and perhaps rightly) idealists and tend to believe that they can achieve more than is actually practicable. The dilemma here is that this always leads to feelings of inadequacy. Teachers must recognize what it is and what it is not possible to achieve effectively and efficiently in that time. The time has now come to look at the activities of the class very carefully in order to decide what is traditional and necessary (e.g. register keeping) and what is traditional and unnecessary, perhaps long queues of children waiting for attention. If children are allowed, they will demand and receive the teacher's attention. In classrooms where they have learned greater independence through learning to use each other as a resource as well as the teacher, they respect the teacher's need to get on with his or her job (Dunne and Bennett, 1990).

This aside, there is other evidence (e.g. Bennett and Kell, 1989) that time is wasted because teachers:

- are not always clear what they want children to get out of activities, i.e. their teaching intentions (Calderhead, 1984); and
- do not then share intentions clearly with the children, putting children in the position of perhaps spending more time working out what the teacher wants than in accomplishing learning (Cullingford, 1991).

Cullingford (1991: 18) asked children about their understanding of classroom life and of what teachers expected of them.

Overwhelmingly, the children suggested that teachers' intentions were related to the *activities* being completed correctly rather than *intentions* related to learning. This is a common finding in other research and almost certainly relates to teachers feeling time pressures to get through as much as possible. There is other evidence, as already shown, from a wealth of sources (e.g. Ausubel *et al.*, 1978; Bruner, 1990; Holt, 1991) that children learn more effectively when they understand what it is they are intended to learn. Much explanation time would undoubtedly be saved by discussing with the children what the intended learning outcomes are of any tasks presented either to the whole class or a variety of group arrangements. It is also vital to ensure that some time is planned for feedback with the children in which they review what they have achieved and the teacher and children together identify present learning and future learning needs. Such interaction is vital for, while time is important, we do need to keep in mind that 'the quality of learning time is more important than time itself' (Jones and Jones, 1986: 242).

Jones and Jones (1986) also offer a useful list of suggestions for saving time which, with a few additions, neatly sums up much of the foregoing discussion:

- Arranging the room for efficient and necessary movement.
- Daily timetables (for groups, class or individuals) are displayed and changes discussed each day.
- The resources and materials are ready for each session or organized in such a way that they are accessible without time wasting.
- Children are clear about what they have to do before they move off to tasks.
- Grouping is organized appropriate to the task.
- The teacher is clear what his or her role is going to be and makes this clear to the children.
- The teacher does not do fundamental tasks which can be done by children but concentrates on teaching.
- Children are periodically reminded of key procedures associated with their activities.
- Children are given step-by-step instructions.
- Transition activities are developed to ensure the day runs smoothly.

Farrell (1989, p. 54) explains how she made significantly more time to teach by giving her 7-year-olds (whom she calls 'students' as in American terminology) responsibility for basic jobs around the classroom and gradually extended it to quite sophisticated peer tutoring. She reports:

> I've used class leaders for several years and I've never had a student who couldn't do the job or didn't enjoy being in charge. Shy students blossom; aggressive ones become more cooperative. All students benefit from having the chance to shine.

The message is clear, teachers must stop doing things for the children which children can adequately do for themselves – and thrive on doing – but should train and teach them to do tasks by the highest possible standards so that everyone is satisfied with the outcomes.

While classes have so many children to one teacher, the 'time-filler' activity may well be a necessity. But what are these and are they really reinforcing or consolidating previous learning or are they simply a 'waste of time'? Teachers need perhaps first of all to admit they are time-fillers and acknowledge that they are unlikely to provide new learning for the children. Accepting that they may need to be provided to free teachers to work more intensively with other children, how can such activities be made to work for children's learning and motivation? There are many useful practical teachers books currently available with a wealth of suggestions and photocopiable resources. Children love doing dot-to-dot sheets which can be numbered according to various tables, rather than the usual straightforward ordinal number and these offer a gentle challenge, as does folding a piece of paper in a number of sections and then drawing a different handwriting pattern in each section. Using a favourite book (or chapter of a book) to find words having the same beginning or ending letter as the child's name, is also a 'filler' which children enjoy in small doses.

Putting two classes together for watching a video or television programme or listening to a radio programme, is an acknow-ledged way of freeing at least one teacher for a short time and the children may benefit socially by being included within the activities of another class and its teacher. Singing practice times can also free most of a school staff either for brief meetings, for planning or for working with individual children. Known in advance, these can be useful times for planning to hear a few children read for diagnostic purposes.

Although the classroom needs to be a flexible environment, constant change for change's sake will only confuse everyone and waste time. If the classroom appears to need rearranging and routines re-establishing every few days, teachers should stop to question why this is occurring: a well-organized classroom should, after all, only need managing, once the basic organizational system is in place. A balance needs to be achieved between constant changes and ensuring appropriate changes for obsolete, time-wasting systems.

At this point, it may be worth asking, how did you, the reader, find time to get through this book? What else are you not doing and why did this appear more important or necessary? Perhaps you can even congratulate yourself for gaining the time!

### Time beyond the children's day

Primary teachers now give as much time out of school as in school to preparing work, planning and doing the myriad of things vital to ensure learning for a class of primary children. Difficult though it may be, some personal time must be maintained and striking out a few evenings and weekend days in a diary should be a feature of every week. Writing 'TTT session' – Taking Time to Think – and not allowing yourself or anyone else to replace that time is vital. Perhaps the most difficult word to adopt, with both children and other adults, is 'No'.

Conscientiousness often leads teachers into a cycle of self-reproach for the unachieved. Try not to waste time and emotional energy in beating yourself with a big stick at the end of each day, agonizing over what you have *not* done. Teachers must note those things which clearly have been achieved. These will often become more evident with sound planning, clear intentions and proactive approaches.

Finally, the time has perhaps now come for primary teachers to speak out clearly in favour of non-contact time, as available to secondary colleagues, for without it the kind of proactive decision making epitomized throughout this book may unfortunately become the aspect to be jettisoned.

# 6

# Deploying adult help effectively in the classroom: Delegation and responsibility

Organizing and managing the learning environment of the primary child demands very particular skills of the teacher, as we have already explored. A parallel ability of being able to work with other adults in the classroom in promoting children's learning is also a skill worth developing, for not only does it have the potential to extend the learning opportunities of the children but can also serve to increase teaching and learning time and offer support. As the teaching role is often a lonely one in terms of other adult relationships, many teachers welcome a range of adults into the classroom as helpers but, as every teacher knows, this type of assistance raises other managerial aspects of utilizing effectively this human resource. Surprisingly, there appears to be little formally written on the roles of other adults in the classroom, and so the theory behind practice is somewhat limited.

One vitally important point to make early is *all visitors to the classroom must be introduced to the children.* 'Stranger danger' messages in relation to the out-of-school world must be supported inside and children should not be expected to communicate with strangers in the classroom unless the teacher's seal of approval is given through a brief introduction.

## Who will provide classroom help?

Assistance is likely to be available from several different sources, some of which will be deliberately budgeted for or engineered within the school context and others given on a voluntary basis. Potential helpers, both professional and voluntary, are likely to include:

- other teachers with a peripatetic role within the school;
- advisory teachers and advisers;
- others teachers with a subject-specific role;
- other teachers perhaps in parallel classes or adjacent classes;
- the headteacher or deputy (particularly if they are without their own class responsibility);
- supply teachers;
- people from outside agencies such as educational psychologists, speech therapists, a school nurse or children's librarian;
- instructors, such as bilingual support or swimming instructors;
- home liaison personnel;
- nursery nurses;
- ancillaries or welfare assistants;
- school meals personnel and caretakers;
- parents/guardians and other relatives, e.g. grandparents;
- governors;
- other children of the same age or older pupils;
- specific visitors, e.g. a local artist or craftsman invited in for a particular purpose, policemen or women, firemen or women;
- students (whether student teachers, nursery nurses, sixth-formers and/or those gaining work experience);
- college/university tutors;
- researchers;
- general 'visitors', perhaps teachers from other schools, overseas visitors, and such like.

Class teachers can find themselves dealing with all of these people or only a selected few. It is worth stopping for a moment to list the people available permanently or periodically to help in your own classroom. If helpers are few, are there other people you could involve? What would be your reason for doing so? If helpers are many, are you able to use them all equally effectively, albeit differently? If not, could their assistance be better distributed during the day, week or term – and how?

## The roles of other teachers in the classroom

Other teachers often constitute the most efficient source of help for they have a similar training and tend to cue into other teachers' classrooms and needs very quickly. However, for similar reasons, they are also sometimes seen to be the greatest threat, particularly to new teachers. It is well worth swallowing all uncomfortable feelings in the short term and using any opportunity provided to work with colleagues for the advantages of sharing information about children and the various activities undertaken is invaluable, even to experienced teachers. Those who work in open-plan, team-taught situations frequently find that, after an initial period of uncertainty, the advantages of having other adults around far outweigh the disadvantages – even if it is only someone else to laugh with or pull a face to when things do not go as planned!

In open-plan schools, it was originally intended that children and teachers should gain by sharing different teachers' expertise. A base of four classes with four teachers with different curriculum strengths, working in a team, all of whom know the children's needs, could well provide a superb opportunity for subject teaching within an overall framework of knowledge and cooperation.

Sharing the planning for, and assessment of, children's learning as well as co-teaching, can make all aspects easier and quicker on a 'two-heads-are-better-than-one' basis though, of course, the relationship between the teachers needs to be positive. Inspiration often comes in bouncing ideas off someone else and self-esteem is raised in helping someone else similarly. Having to verbalize implicit thoughts on a teaching or learning process helps in developing one's own stance.

Teachers within the school also need to decide as a team what are the most useful ways of disseminating help to each other. If the peripatetic teacher is full-time but there are 10 classes within the schools, do some classes have more need of that kind of help than others or should the time be divided equally? Perhaps that teacher will be used to release teachers with subject expertise to work with other classes, a useful strategy for gaining the most from subject specialists, provided the specialists' own classes do not miss out too significantly on contact time with their own teacher.

Should the assisting teacher in a specific classroom work alongside the class teacher in a parallel role? Should he or she take over the class, releasing the class teacher to work with some children intensively for a given period? Or should the assisting teacher take aside particular individuals or groups for specific teaching? Certain curriculum aspects will demand one role and others another: hearing individual children read for diagnostic or assessment purposes may require the class teacher to be released from class responsibility for a reasonable period, whereas group teaching sessions will benefit from having another teacher in a general or specific classroom support role.

Senior teachers, including the head, may well need an invitation into the classroom, for many are reluctant to come without. Most heads, busy as they are, appreciate opportunities to work in classrooms and acquaint themselves with the children and their needs as well as get a general feel for the teacher's organization and management of the classroom. Even if the visit is perfunctory and unannounced, one child is usually ready to read a story, or show an experiment, or discuss current work, and heads should be made to feel that they are, like others, welcome.

## Using teachers' curriculum expertise

Older primary children, whose own knowledge and skills are moving forward in leaps and bounds, will undoubtedly benefit from being able to work with other teachers in the school with specific expertises. This will not only give them insight into secondary school methods (about which many 10- and 11-year-olds become quite anxious: Cullingford, 1991), but also ensure the greatest quality in subject teaching. The disadvantages are that if a particular class is undertaking a specific topic focus, it may be difficult for the specialist teacher to undertake related activities. Where whole school topics are used or year groups have been allocated specific foci, this may be less problematic, though it will require liaison between teachers over content, processes and skills necessary for a particular class. This time may well be cancelled out by the regular class teacher (who will be expert in another area) not having to spend precious out-of-school hours in hunting out ideas, information and resources for that particular subject, on the assumption that it is quicker to work from the known than the unknown. Another disadvantage is that the teacher who knows his or her own class best could well relinquish the children to someone who knows them less well for quite a proportion of each week, and therefore the timetable, already discussed in Chapter 5, would need to be scrutinized for balance. Classes whose relationship balances are tenuous may well find working with another teacher unsettling; equally, though, some children may find a different teaching style a refreshing challenge. Where single class situations are the norm, such subject work could be undertaken on a teacher exchange basis (exchanging class for class and expertise for expertise) or use the time of a peripatetic full- or part-time teacher.

Subject co-ordinators are used in many schools to lead staff seminars on a curriculum area, encouraging other teachers to share their knowledge and skills for the benefit of the children. Scarcity of time renders this of limited value given that there are nine main curriculum areas plus religious education each term. Other schools use their co-ordinators to produce packs of suitable ideas and materials for various age groups and this has the advantage of being very flexible, accessible and saving other teachers' time. Such packs are a boon provided the compilers have considered and detailed for users not only the content of the subject but the rationale for the teaching of the various skills and processes: why a particular element is useful and how the stages develop children's understanding progressively. Many schemes suffer similarly, giving a range of exciting activities but never telling teachers *why* these are important to the full implementation of the subject.

Sharing classes for storytelling, singing, television, radio or similar sessions can free some teachers from full class responsibility for short periods. Provided adequate space is available and children have sufficient individual space, it can give precious individual or group time for a few children and a teacher and, on a regular basis, can provide a steady flow of flexible time. The receiving teacher, however, does need a full repertoire of skills (see earlier chapters) to hold the attention of such a large group. Irrespective of the age of the children, the session should be no longer than 20 minutes if children are to view it as an exciting and interesting time and minimize discipline problems.

## Other uses of professional support

Personal and professional support, as well as actual classroom assistance, is also valuable. New teachers to a school should have a mentor attached to them, someone to whom they can turn for an occasional informal chat about progress or who can help with difficult children, classroom organization and management issues or general professional development. We are usually part-way to solving a problem if its existence is recognized. Teachers can become very insular in their own classrooms and sometimes very unhappy because they feel that it is they alone who have problems with certain children or certain curriculum aspects. Encouraging a staffroom atmosphere where issues are raised and professional advice sought, helps many teachers to acknowledge that their problems are common professional dilemmas and it might be that these should be noted and raised occasionally at staff meetings for open discussion and potential resolution. The whole school acting together on, for example, behavioural or racial issues, is not only supportive but vital for the consistency of the messages given and received by all (see Davey, 1983; Westmacott and Cameron, 1988).

## Sending children to other adults

A general discipline response in schools is to send a child out of the classroom for a moment or to the head or senior teacher. On the whole, unless this is the agreed policy within the school for a particularly difficult child, this is rarely beneficial to anyone. Moreover, it could be dangerous, for once the teacher–child relationship has disintegrated to that extent, the child may well decide to remove him or herself from the school altogether at a time when the teacher is, in fact, legally responsible for the child's welfare. If such dismissals happen frequently, it is likely that the teacher–child relationship has broken down and, in a sense, the teacher has 'lost'. The notion of 'time-out' for difficult children can and should occur in the context of the classroom where, at an appropriate moment, after a period of cooling off, the teacher can talk to the child and regain the footing of a satisfactory relationship. In other circumstances, it may be necessary and safer to send a reliable child with a message asking the head or other colleague for immediate assistance. The type of children who require this kind of attention are, fortunately, rare and teachers usually have a well-defined procedure for necessary action. Does your school have such a system?

## Supply teachers

Being a supply teacher is, is many ways, an unenviable role yet invaluable in today's primary schools. Their scarcity would suggest that schools and teachers should do everything to help supply teachers to settle down quickly, yet the obverse is often the case (Trotter and Wragg, 1990). Because the classroom is very much the domain of a particular teacher and class of children, it can be quite difficult for an outsider to understand all the nuances of the context. Well-displayed, fully labelled resources and materials can help from an organizational point, but the supply teacher's management style may be very different and children (as Alan Ahlberg, 1984, astutely recognizes in his poem, 'The Supply Teacher') will sometimes react quite anxiously to the new, albeit temporary, system.

Children should *always* be given the name of the supply teacher and an explanation of his or her presence – as before, let them in on the secrets as they can only respond appropriately if they have such information and knowledge. Plans for the term, week and day should be shared with the supply teacher either verbally or, more likely, in writing. The timetable will be available on the noticeboard but it is as well to have a spare ready. Have plenty of children's name lists around so activities can be monitored for each child. Make a list of the general rules of the classroom (perhaps written and supplied by the children) to include such aspects as whether children ask before going to the toilet, can any number go at once, where do they put finished work (if this is not obvious), are they allowed to use rubbers, what are the procedures for leaving the room, and so on. More personal details like arrangements to acquire a cup of coffee or where to put one's coat are welcoming and welcomed, together with a list of staff names. If all these are enclosed within a pocket folder, a gentle reassuring message (using the person's name rather than 'Supply Teacher') can be included with a note of thanks – it is useful to have such information prepared in anticipation of an emergency. Appropriate gestures may well mean future success in acquiring the services of the supply teacher.

*Ancillaries, nursery nurses and support instructors*

If you are lucky enough to have a full-time nursery nurse or ancillary working with you, it is important from the outset to be clear about the similarities and differences in the jobs undertaken. Each person brings different skills to the classroom and these can only be used efficiently if they are known and acknowledged. At least part of an ancillary or nursery nurse role may be related to organizational matters, perhaps mixing paints, cutting papers and ensuring that the general resources and materials are readily available, thus ensuring teacher's time for teaching is maximized. Opportunities to undertake these aspects should be carefully planned in relation to what else is happening in the classroom, for example, while the teacher is involved in whole class teaching, so that when children are working in groups or as individuals the ancillary or nursery nurse is free from organizational tasks and able to work towards meeting learning needs (see Brown and Cleave, 1991). Much time is wasted by non-teaching personnel sitting listening to teachers' discussions with children (often about administrative issues) which serve little useful purpose and diminish the assistant's influence.

## Caretaker and cleaners

While these people may not be directly involved with the children in the school day, their contribution to the classroom as a learning environment should never be underestimated: a good caretaker and cleaners, who recognize and appreciate the classroom as an orderly working environment and are keen to do their best for the school (Haigh, 1991), are a boon to any class teacher. But equally, class teachers and children should play their part in ensuring that, at the end of the day, the classroom is left in such a condition that caretaker and cleaners can also fulfil their roles effectively. Giving preliminary notice about using potentially messy materials such as clay will enable the caretaker and cleaner to plan their work schedules more effectively. Explaining briefly the benefits of using different mediums with children, with an assurance that children will be expected to clean up satisfactorily, will go a long way to fostering goodwill and dispelling the caretaker's anxieties.

## The involvement of parents and governors

With the home and community now emphasized partners in schooling, parents and governors rightly have a significant role. Parents have been variously seen over the last 30 years as helpers, supporters, providers, collaborators, participators and, more recently, partners in the processes of their children's learning and now, under The Parents' Charter (1991), have rights and responsibilities for education. Governors by law determine much of what happens in school and in fulfilling their duties appropriately they will need an understanding of how teachers use their training and skills in ensuring a good-quality education for children.

*Parent helpers* in the classroom have a wide range of backgrounds and different perspectives on school, some having enjoyed their own educational experiences, though some may bring quite impoverished views. Most remember mainly the pencil and paper type learning which characterized most secondary schooling in previous years and, therefore, bring the same expectations of children's involvement in tasks and are sometimes quite disturbed by the noisier, more active classrooms of today's teaching methods.

In encouraging parental help, be clear about what forms of help are being offered and what is needed. Many parents and other such adults prefer doing organizational tasks, some come particularly to work with the children. Parents with only minimal knowledge of current schooling will need help in, for example, understanding what children learn from practical tasks or drafting and redrafting their writing. Parents' work groups, formed for the purpose of making equipment such as maths or reading games, or covering and labelling resources, are preferred by those who are unsure about working with children.

Some schools discourage parents from helping in their own child's class but welcome them in other classes. This is very much a matter for school policy and the general staff views. However, many parents want to help because they want to see inside the school life of their child mainly denied to them within this kind of restriction. Teachers too can 'gain a better understanding of a particular child ... by increasing the communication between themselves and a parent' (Gillespie, 1988: 95).

Some children relish their parents helping in school: others deplore it. It is worth gauging the reactions of the child to their parent's participation and encouraging them to discuss how they feel. One of my own sons was disturbed for quite the opposite reason: because I am a teacher myself, I was unable to help in his school as other mothers did and he passed many months feeling very deprived and rather angry at my seeming unwillingness to help in his class. Discussion and explanation was only moderately helpful, but eventually he became reasonably satisfied with a different kind of involvement, at home – I made all the costumes for their next concert!

Evening sessions, which many schools run for parents on curriculum issues such as special needs, can often inspire a parent who may have previously felt inadequate to help. Letters home with requests for classroom assistance are most successful if they list some of the activities which helpers might undertake or which would be most useful to the school and also give an indication of the potential time commitment, e.g. one afternoon a week.

*Governors* will appreciate the opportunity to be involved in the work of different classes in order to get a feel for the school and its working practices in order to inform decisions at governors' meetings and to support the head and staff in the daily administration. Some prefer to come as visitors rather than helpers, but can often be persuaded to sit and talk to a group of children and usually enjoy doing so.

### Children as helpers

Peer tutoring was discussed in Chapter 5. In some schools, older children are used as tutors for younger children and a number of different pieces of research into this older peer tutoring have found it to be extremely successful, particularly in relation to reading (Topping, 1987). Schools might also consider older children helping younger ones with the transitional stages of writing or in developing fluid handwriting skills. Older children writing stories for younger ones was particularly successful in my own school, where we paired an older and a younger child periodically to work at the development of a story to meet the younger child's needs. In addition to learning about copyright and the role of the author, older children learned skills of interviewing, note-taking, drafting and redrafting, illustration, presentation and writing for a specific audience. They developed personal and social skills in relating to a younger child and empathizing with their needs for story characters and content. The interaction of the two classes became a highlight of the week for both, and the teachers were able to observe children in a different setting and assess other aspects of learning.

## Specific visitors with a purpose

Inviting in local people is the first step in bringing into school a sense of community and citizenship, so much a part of modern education. The notion of learning through modelling is as old as humanity, yet it is not necessarily emphasized in schools. Seeing a craftsman at work and then attempting to employ some of the skills observed for yourself, is fascinating for children and adults alike. Showing that adults are prepared to persevere towards a goal is useful practical learning. Learning about public services – the police, ambulance service and fire brigade – puts children in touch with the real world and its needs. Other adults in the classroom showing that they are readers, writers or artists encourages children to see purpose in their own learning. The oral tradition and the power of story for the transmission of information and ideas is worthwhile remembering, as this is a classic way of 'telling' while interacting meaningfully with the learner (Egan, 1988). Many otherwise reluctant classroom visitors may well be happy recalling features of their own lives, particularly schooldays, and most children will be enthralled by an impromptu history session.

Places such as the local library, police station or health centre mostly welcome contact with the children either in schools or in their locations and many are delighted to have displays of children's activities either following visits or for community liaison and

*Inviting in local people is the first step in bringing into school a sense of community and citizenship, so much a part of modern education.*

information purposes. Would it be worthwhile making such contacts in your school? Should it be a whole school decision or can individuals take the initiative? What would be the benefits to the children? What would be the benefits to the service?

### Students and tutors

Students can bring a breath of fresh air into any classroom and working with a less experienced colleague gives many teachers added confidence, though at the expense of having to spend time discussing practice. With teacher education increasingly moving into the school context, organization and management gain even greater importance as the classroom structure will need to support one or more students as well as the teacher and children. Tutors from local higher education institutions will also provide a source of information and support for teachers and students as they bring experience of a variety of other classroom situations with them, and many teachers use the opportunity to discuss class-related issues with the tutor and students together in a training partnership. Where two students, the teacher and a tutor work together, this can be a powerful force for really evaluating classroom practices and children's learning (see Everton and Impey, 1990). Depending on the period of time within their courses, students may only be able to take small groups or have responsibility for the whole class and though time will be needed to discuss classroom events and children's learning, having students normally means teachers, gain time and opportunity to work more closely with individuals and/ or groups of children. Time spent in other classes usually adds a useful dimension.

## Making the most of classroom assistance

The actual distribution of help across the year is likely to be varied, with some being regularly provided within the daily or weekly timetable and other types occurring only once or twice in the year, for example, advisory teacher support. Whether it is sustained, intermittent or one-off, efforts must be made to ensure that it benefits all the people involved, especially the children. A few factors are paramount: planning, communicating, using people's skills and interests, modelling certain behaviours, delegating, giving feedback, monitoring and evaluating. For the sake of convenience, all those likely to assist in the classroom will, from now on, be called 'helpers'.

### Planning

It is very difficult to plan effectively the use of other people's time 'off-the-cuff' in a busy classroom. Be clear in the long and short term, by use of the prepared plans for the term and week:

- When is help needed?
- What kind of help?
- For how long?

Balance this with known times of assistance (when you are allocated support teacher or ancillary time) and attempt to fill the gaps. It is preferable to have helpers in for one really useful hour than have them hanging around ineffectually.

Try not to have too many people on the same day for, rather than being a help, this can mean that the children's attention is divided between a range of adults and the general cohesion is lost. Identify those times within your timetable where you and the children will genuinely require help; for example, you may decide to devote half a morning to science investigations, which will be followed after play by all the children being involved in recording and

*Helpers should, like the children, be clear about what they are doing, why they are doing it and what benefits it has to the children and the teacher.*

communicating the results. Clearly, another one or two adults, who are familiar with what you are intending, could help significantly both in monitoring the children's investigations, proffering suggestions for other strategies and in helping with the various ways in which the results may be presented.

### Communicating

Helpers should, like the children, be clear about what they are doing, why they are doing it and what benefits it has to the children and the teacher. The children should also be told what the adult's role is and how the children are expected to interact and behave. Many voluntary helpers need encouragement in not doing tasks for the children but in helping children themselves achieve: some children will feign inability if they believe the adult will do the task for them. If any children leave the room to work with a helper, allow them the opportunity (however brief) to share experiences with others when they return and vice versa.

Finding time to communicate the task intentions and outcomes is difficult and meeting helpers outside classroom time to plan is time-consuming though probably vital, particularly early in the relationship. Written communication at any stage is necessary because verbal exchanges can be misunderstood or forgotten and written ones can be referred to again and again. These should be simple, perhaps point out what are the objectives for the task – for example, 'To write out a poem in order to practise a flowing style of handwriting' – and how this may be evaluated for success – 'Observe the children's pencil grip. Do they look comfortable?' If you want the helper to note something about a particular child in the group or something about the task itself, most voluntary helpers would prefer to have some kind of checklist, though other professionals may prefer undertaking this for themselves. Seeing something through to completion gives satisfaction to helpers. Knowing what the individual or group are to do once this task is satisfactorily completed is also vital information.

A well-organized classroom gives helpers (and children) confidence in accessing materials which they can then replace without embarrassment or interrupting the teacher. Labelling things with pictures is useful, particularly for younger children, but will also help parents who may not always be familiar with such terms as 'Probability resources' or 'Logiblocs' and those helpers whose mother tongue is other than English. Teacher-made games should have a written explanation of the rules on the back and a note of what learning is intended so that helpers can share this information with the children.

## Using helpers' present skills and interests

Find out early what helpers are good at: we all perform better when we are doing what is comfortable and about which we feel reasonably confident. Early in the process, classroom helpers will appreciate feeling that they have been invited or welcomed into the classroom because they have something special to offer. If a parent has expressed an interest in doing cookery with children, it would be unfair to ask them to cut paper, mix paints and listen to readers. Those who appreciate being part of children's writing processes could sit with a group presenting their previous activity's outcomes in terms of a story, whereas a parent skilled in the use of computers may well monitor pairs of children working on a word-processing package. Yet another helper may be skilled in helping children create visual images through artwork and could be encouraged to follow this group through the session. There is no harm at all in encouraging them to do some of the more mundane tasks for you to fill in the odd 10 minutes when children are clearing up. Having a list of these jobs on a noticeboard or pinned behind the door would mean they could be undertaken without reference to the teacher once the helper is aware of this system.

### Modelling teaching behaviours

Teachers should conduct themselves at all times by the standards they wish helpers to adopt for, inevitably, others will model themselves on this example in an unfamiliar context. If the teacher is positive with the children, they will be also: if the teacher is calm and relaxed, helpers will adopt this approach also. Offering in-school training, perhaps given by the head, an adviser or class teacher with responsibility for liaison, would be welcomed by many helpers, both other professionals and volunteers. Where a school is small, families of local schools can collaborate in such training. The helpers can determine the agenda in relation to their own perceived needs.

### Delegate

Few primary teachers are good at this, as they know their job so well it seems easier to do things for themselves. However, well-executed delegation is probably the biggest time bonus for everyone in the classroom – and this also means delegating to the children. As Jenks and Kelly (1986: 13–14) observe: 'Delegation is more than just assigning work. It always means making your subordinate accountable for results ... delegation never relieves you of responsibility.' Delegation is certainly a powerful tool, not a way of opting out, and should be used when it is clear that the helper is capable of carrying out the task and reporting on it without recourse to the teacher in between.

### Give feedback

However briefly, having the opportunity for feedback of some kind makes people feel valued. Listening to what the helper has to say rather than questioning probably elicits the most useful information. It is better to wait until the children have left before launching in on the day's anecdotes! Showing appreciation by the occasional 'Thank you' card, particularly done by the children, is valuable. If you want the helper to return, say you look forward to seeing them on x day at x time – and mean it.

## Monitor and evaluate the process

If things did not go as intended, was it something in the planning, communication, helper's role/approach, lack of clarity of teacher's intentions or a child-related factor which created the difficulty, or was it something outside anyone's control? Some parent helpers flounder simply because they do not understand the internal language of the classroom and things can be taken very literally which actually have far deeper meaning. Even a simple 'Tidy away now' can mean many things beyond that: put the books in the middle of the table, put the pencil pots on the cupboard, push your chairs under without scraping, don't kick the person next to you and come and sit on the carpet. The classroom abounds with such examples.

## The pros and cons of helpers in the classroom

Opening up the primary classroom is probably the most advantageous way of showing everyone the complexities of its internal structures, the quality of teacher–children relationships and the learning environment. Teachers who welcome regular or intermittent helpers will, all things considered, have more time for the children as individuals and as groups. In-school teacher exchanges may well allow greater use of expertise in the subject curriculum. Teachers opening up their classes to others often discover a wonderful support system hitherto unrecognized.

Like teachers learning through teaching, outside helpers in the classroom will inevitably gain insights into the teaching and learning processes inherent within each classroom situation and may then be ready to help counteract some of the more negative statements frequently propounded by politicians and the media.

The benefits are, therefore, two-way. Much research – especially with younger children – has made it clear that parents and teachers have much to learn from each other, which will ultimately benefit the children and the home–school relationship. Children will be exposed to the wider social contexts of learning, have different opportunities to practise social skills, particularly ways of relating to different people and see adults cooperating and collaborating in a variety of ways. Culturally, having different groups of people working in the classroom can broaden children's horizons and break down stereotyped images. As primary staff are still predominantly female, having males in the classroom can help to ensure a greater balance between gendered views!

All helpers, especially voluntary ones, need to ensure that they respect the confidentiality of some aspects of classroom and school life. It would be quite unacceptable for helpers to discuss individual children's progress with others outside the school, for example, but they may not recognize this without it being pointed out. Schools need to have clear guidelines for all helpers, written in a sensitive and sympathetic style. Emphasis should be given to differences in children's and teachers' approaches to tasks, the range of outcomes and their equal acceptability. Children may, unless the helper's role is clear, try to play one adult off against the other. Communicating the helper's and children's roles quite clearly to everyone can overcome this.

Parent and family helpers can be educationalists' most vociferous allies, as they can be encouraged to understand the value of such activities as exploratory play in the classroom and opportunities for children's discussion and purposeful talk. They will vouch for the intensity of the teacher's role and the variety of children's approaches to tasks, though they will only be able to do this if they have been made part of the overall plans for the day and encouraged to see where the various parts fit.

If teachers are to have a wider expertise role within the school and share their classes with others, their classroom organization and management strategies must be equally clear to others who may, periodically, work there. Standards and expectations of activities and behaviour will need to be articulated and manifested in the way children generally go about their daily tasks. On-going monitoring and a periodic reassessment of the learning environment will be beneficial to the class teacher, children and those, described above, who contribute on a full- or part-time basis to the classroom processes. This is the focus of Chapter 7.

# 7

## *Evaluating classroom organization and management*

> As practising teachers and student-teachers frequently testify, what they learn through teaching in the classroom is the most important single factor in their personal and professional development (Wenham, 1991: 237).

As Wenham implies, teachers' own learning is a vital feature of classroom life and teachers must engage in analysis and reflection (Hull *et al.*, 1985). Time connotations are, unfortunately, unavoidable. In order to know *how* to utilize time and other resources more effectively, it is necessary to *use* some time to find out how these are currently used and there is really no alternative.

Undoubtedly, the most important aspect of classroom life is monitoring and evaluating children's progress and attainment – just the features of the National Curriculum which have generated the need for teachers to review their classroom management and organization in depth. Children's opportunities to learn and the teachers' opportunities to follow up teaching with any form of assessment, however, will depend on many other classroom factors themselves being critically evaluated and it is these with which this book is primarily concerned.

In this chapter, therefore, we will look first at some of the underlying issues regarding monitoring and evaluating practice, which will lead into raising questions about reasons for analysing the classroom as a learning environment and potential ways of undertaking classroom analysis. The final section draws on the contents of all earlier chapters and gives a very few practical examples of those aspects which will benefit from class teachers' occasional scrutiny, namely the role of the teacher, the physical context of the classroom, children and learning, time use and working with other adults.

## Analysing classroom practice

Studies such as those undertaken by Mortimore *et al.* (1988) and Galton *et al.* (1980) have found that though the teacher's day is full of interactions with children, many of these are low-level, administrative and managerial contacts, related to routine matters, rather than interactions related to higher level teaching and learning. Mortimore's study found enormous variety in the time spent in actual teaching and Galton's ORACLE study found that whereas the teachers were in almost constant contact with children during the day, most children had very little contact with the teacher. Do these situations still apply now? If they do, what does this mean to the 'entitlement curriculum'?

Many teachers have, as a result of the National Curriculum and assessment procedures, had to reappraise and change existing practice to accommodate all that is required. To investigate the current situation, I shadowed four teachers in classrooms across the 6–11 years age range for a day each in order to monitor various aspects such as time use, interactions, types of teaching undertaken and children's contributions to the day. The results were interesting and enlightening and, to a certain extent, still reflect the findings of earlier studies.

The average contact day with children appeared to be some 268 minutes (the classes varied by only 3 minutes either way). Within this time, however, there were significant differences in the amount of time spent in actual teaching – sustained contact with class, group or individuals – and that spent on administrative and functional managerial aspects. Administration constituted registration, money collection, discussing letters sent home to parents and so on; managerial aspects related to the everyday routines of material provision, stopping and starting sessions, giving instructions and generally prompting the completion of children's tasks and outcomes.

Even given that most classroom research suffers from the fact that only certain days can be sampled and, inevitably, days are different depending on the 'fixed' elements in the general timetable, the differences were quite prominent. Teaching time with the whole class varied from 18 to 77 minutes, group teaching from 21 to 76 minutes, administration from 20 to 38 minutes and functional managerial aspects from 58 to 76 minutes. Together the administration and managerial aspects formed between 29 and 42.5 per cent of the school day. The year group of the classes (2–6) was not necessarily significant, with one infant teacher spending the most whole class teaching time and an upper junior teacher the least, perhaps reflecting the vast differences in teaching style and approaches to children's learning (or variations within the timetabled day). The maximum time in any class during which individual children contributed to whole class discussion was 11 minutes – the least 4 minutes – though children were involved in peer discussions centred around their activities between 50 and 95 per cent of the total time during group tasks. Up to four subject areas were identifiable in the day, with writing occupying a major portion of children's time in all classes (between 35 and 95 per cent), though on different aspects of curriculum: a support for the discussion in Chapter 5 relating to basic skills. In none of the classes was actual collaborative work, described in Chapter 4, undertaken, though group reading was a feature of a year 6 class. Two classes had helpers for an average of 1 hour in the day of the visits. Only between 1 and 3 minutes was spent in any of the classes on disciplinary matters and then mostly with individuals representing, at least in this sample, the quality of the relationships and underlying rule structures these teachers had with their classes. Alexander and co-workers' (1992) working party has similarly commented upon the high quality of relationships in primary classrooms.

The teachers were generally surprised by the findings from this shadowing activity, particularly in as much as they certainly *felt* they were busy teaching all day and children were learning a majority of the time. The teachers did feel, however, that much of this was what might be called 'social learning', e.g. learning to get on with others, share equipment, learn independence and so on. Curriculum learning intentions were not always in sharp focus and in no classroom were these shared with the children; rather, children were told what to do and how to do it but not why. All teachers wanted genuinely to explore ways in which the balance of the day might be changed. This is at the heart of both the monitoring process and proactive teaching. As Day *et al.* (1987: Ch. 5) assert, observation in one's own classroom of one's own behaviours is a must in order for teachers to reflect on their professional development.

Potential opportunities for analysis and evaluation already exist within the context of every teacher's current teaching and learning plans and evaluation needs to become a general part of classroom events rather than something additional. As with learning, sharing intentions about monitoring and evaluating with the children will enable them to do some of it for themselves. For example, primary children are well used to monitoring such activities as how many birds visit the bird table in a given period during a day or week. An equally valid learning experience would be for them to monitor the use of a classroom bay, perhaps noting at given times each day, over one or more weeks (depending on the age of the children and what information is required), how many people are working there and for what purpose. A topic about classrooms, their use and functions, would readily incorporate investigating the curriculum, systems, children's learning, friendships, seating arrangements, learning resources and a wealth of other issues.

## Reasons for monitoring

As the shadowing process reveals, knowing *what* is actually happening – not what is *thought* to be happening – in classrooms can reveal very differing features. A main reason for monitoring, therefore, is to heighten class teachers' awareness of what is actually occurring in the day-to-day organization and management of their own classrooms and allow opportunities for considering:

- the improvement of practice;
- the improvement of understanding of practice by practitioners;
- the improvement of the situation in which practice takes place (Carr and Kemmis, 1986: 165).

Analysis of the classroom learning environment mainly occurs for the purposes of establishing what is presently happening which is effective and what aspects are in need of a revision or minor adjustment. As an example, a teacher who constantly had problems with children jostling each other every time they were asked to sit on the carpet, almost immediately recognized that two large bean-bags were the source of contention and setting minor rules for their use resolved the difficulty. As Kyriacou (1991: 126) points out: 'Change does not mean that your previous practice was wrong', merely that something different or additional is perhaps required – it was not wrong to supply the bean-bags but necessary to discuss their use. While making efforts to interpret objectively what

*Analysis of the classroom learning environment mainly occurs for the purposes of establishing what is presently happening that is effective and what aspects are in need of revision or minor adjustment.*

is seen, teachers are able to use intuition and insight into both the children and classroom context, something which formal researchers cannot do.

Through monitoring and evaluating the quality of the teacher's and children's experiences in the classroom, it will be possible to identify teachers' needs and make decisions as to necessary in-service education which, now that it lies almost wholly within schools' delegated budgets, has far more questions raised over its use. Something as simple as making decisions about which books would encourage members of staff to read and reflect on classroom practice may evolve from evaluation experiences.

Like everything we do, people will only see a need for aspects of monitoring and evaluation if it stems from a genuine personal desire to discover something useful; therefore, a golden rule is for individual teachers to identify aspects which are of real concern to them. This means, as indicated very early in this book, not accepting those things which continually cause irritation and stress but acknowledging them and examining what might be done. If children form frequent queues around the teacher, what is the reason for this? What is it the children need? Could they satisfy that need in some other way? Is the teacher creating a dependency model by insisting on seeing every piece of work at all stages? Or are the children unclear about their own levels of responsibility for tasks undertaken? However, only the teacher in that classroom will be able to identify the causes and an important feature of classroom evaluation is in identifying and analysing the antecedents to unwanted behaviours or events. This also applies to individual children's unacceptable behaviour where knowledge of antecedents will give the teacher a head start in anticipating and deflecting unwanted outcomes (Docking, 1990).

The effectiveness of change will also need monitoring. An important feature is not to keep making changes for changes sake but, having gone through the process of identifying aspects of concern and making plans to deal with them, scrupulous monitoring is necessary to ensure on-going satisfactory outcomes.

Above all, because schools and classrooms exist to ensure the promotion of children's educational development and learning, the outcomes of any monitoring and evaluation procedures should have children and teachers at their heart. The relationship between the two will always underpin the most effective practice, though its building blocks, as shown in previous chapters, are inevitably the classroom and the way it is organized and managed.

*When to monitor*

Like planning, monitoring and evaluation have long-, medium- and short-term implications. Some facets of classroom life are clearly influenced by that which is 'external' to the single class under consideration, e.g. when assembly occurs in relation to the day, when hall times, video/television opportunities occur, the timing of playtime in relation to assembly time and so on. If these constitute a difficulty to individual classes and teachers, then they need to be raised and discussed by the staff as a whole or, at the very least, with the person who undertakes the school timetabling. It may be that the teaching staff decides to look at independent features of each half-term and the way they act upon different classes with a view to making necessary timetable revisions at a future time.

Medium- and short-term analyses, monitoring and evaluation should occur at almost any time when there appears to be a need to investigate from either a summative or formative baseline, e.g. to check on whether a particular feature of the classroom, the main display area say, operates effectively for the predetermined reasons (summative – will tell you that this is or is not so), or to raise questions about why something occurs, e.g. a particular time of the day appears to be noisier than others (formative – will be diagnostic and lead to knowledge of what might be done).

## Ways and means of monitoring and evaluating

Teachers regularly and deliberately gather information regarding children and activities through note-taking, marking children's work and observing activities. There is also the intuitive, reflexive 'noticing' which takes place, often subconsciously, but which should not be underestimated or ignored. Impressions, provided they are substantiated through analysis and monitoring, are an important part of the teacher's repertoire of techniques.

Gathering the information is only one aspect, however, in as much as the next phase is to make something of the data collected which is usable in promoting quality practices. Because the day and week consist of so many different elements, it is easy to concentrate on too many small things and fail to gain an objective overview: thus one teacher in the shadowing experience felt, because of her own focused involvement with *some* of the class during the day, that *all* children had been involved.

### Gathering data

Information about the classroom as a system can be gathered in at least four main ways:

1 *Observation*: this can be either direct or through audio/video recordings. Systematic observation (Croll, 1986) involves the use of schedules or checklists which are devised by the teacher for the purpose of gathering very specific, focused information, perhaps in a designated time. Informal observation usually consists of recording everything of significance that happens, both the expected and unexpected. Participant observation is also a useful tool for class teachers as it allows for their involvement within the activity. Thompson and Thompson (1984) give many excellent examples of teachers undertaking classroom observations, as does the Open University's *Curriculum in Action* pack (1980).

2 *Discussion*: much can be learned about the way the classroom enables children's learning or otherwise through discussion about the context and progress of activities. Such discussion may take

the form of questioning by the teacher. Like observation, data gathering through discussion can be very structured and geared to establishing quite specific aspects, but it also has an informal function of straightforward teacher–child(ren) dialogue. Much can also be learned about classroom processes and functions by discussion with other involved adults.

3 *Writing*: written plans in themselves should form the basis of daily teaching and learning intentions as well as contain information about classroom management issues – groupings, rearrangement of furniture, resource and materials provision, time available, etc. – and will be monitored and evaluated for their suitability. In support of such written monitoring, teachers need to have a notepad and pen constantly to hand for those vital bits of information which arise all the time. But teachers should also consider keeping a journal in which informal observations, ideas, information about particular aspects of the classroom context can be stored for eventual use if necessary. (Sometimes, just the very act of writing it down aids memory.) It is surprising how often an amalgam of quite incidental anecdotal notes highlights a feature worthy of deeper investigation or answers a query. Children may also be encouraged to write down information about the group in which they worked or whether a particular resource helped them achieve success in a task as in some aspect like design technology or resources borrowed from museum or library services.

4 *Recording*: in terms of the classroom context, probably the best kind of record is that provided through photography. Videos made of classroom practices are invaluable in identifying bottlenecks or underused parts of the room. Photographs/slides also add a temporal quality to daily classroom life and can also be used to remind class and teacher about past events and various forms of room layout for different purposes. If noise levels are under investigation, a tape-recording can equally provide a source of information as to whether, for example, the talk is related to the activities, whether particular children's voices stand out, whether one sex dominates group discussion, whether peer-tutoring situations are actually engendering learning opportunities.

None of these methods is discrete: the teacher may observe a group using a new piece of science equipment and then discuss with the children how it helped them with their activity. The teacher may write notes, perhaps for record-keeping purposes, on children's interactions through watching a video clip of a group activity.

Both qualititative and quantitative approaches will be necessary for different purposes in order to gather and later interpret basic data. Objective strategies include investigating classroom events or situations in terms of:

- frequency,
- duration,
- time use,
- occurrence,
- balance,
- sequence,
- people involved,
- interaction,
- resource use.

In practice, a teacher would be selective in choosing only one or two of these to be used together.

As an example of a straightforward recording and written monitoring procedure, a class teacher was dissatisfied with the children's responses in whole class discussions feeling that they were too brief and too shallow in content. The teacher decided to audio record the next geography session and note both the questions and prompts he used and the children's responses. In listening to the tape later, the teacher realized that in 10 minutes of class discussion, he used no less than 36 questions, many of which were multiple questions in themselves, consisting of two or three questions strung together, and he waited only a few seconds for a child's response, often cutting the child off the minute the crux of the question was answered. Through monitoring this session, the teacher was able, in planning for future class sessions, to think more carefully about the number and type of questions posed to children to elicit learning, as well as ensure that children's answering time more adequately allowed for a fuller response.

All methods require teachers to have:

- a clear purpose and idea of how the information will be obtained and what use it will have;
- time set aside within planning for the particular monitoring aspect to be undertaken (either by teacher, children or other adult) and time for analysis;
- devised all necessary checklists or observation schedules beforehand;

- if necessary, a stopwatch or other timing devise readily available;
- audio-visual equipment, checked and ready, if needed;
- shared the intentions with children, e.g. the teacher or observer having a specific 'signal', such as the wearing of a particular emblem (I used to have a large owl badge) to signify the role of observer rather than interactor.

Many methods of monitoring can be, and would probably benefit from being, a collaborative venture with other colleagues wherever possible, either to facilitate comparison or gain a different perspective. Getting another teacher, student or tutor to be a 'shadow' observer for all or part of a day would be most beneficial to teachers in investigating their own use of class time and teacher/children contributions to the day. Having a volunteer helper make notes on the use of a particular classroom area or monitor the events of a given time in the day may be equally valuable.

Using professional classroom helpers to either take the class while the teacher monitors some aspect of interest or to do the monitoring themselves in a manner predetermined with the class teacher, may ultimately prove to be the best possible utilization of such help if the outcomes assist in identifying classroom practices in which time and effort might be better used.

Whatever the method, it must be simple and fit easily within the teaching day. Choosing between the various possible ways of monitoring will depend on what information is required, the time available and the activities under consideration.

## What aspects can be monitored and evaluated

What is happening? How is it happening? Why is it happening? All three of these questions will constitute the basis for monitoring, analysing and evaluating the classroom as a learning environment and, in common with other very simple statements, they hide a wealth of ideas and information. Both organizational and managerial factors will feature in the processes as well as the relationship between the two. Events, interactions and materials (Croll, 1986: 11) are all worthy foci: all are interrelated and juxtaposed.

The lists of necessary balances, already given in Chapters 1 and 3, constitute the basis for questions to be raised regarding the roles and behaviours of teacher and children in the classroom learning context. Reflection on these aspects is likely to result in a number of questions being generated, all of which will have spin-offs in other areas. Some analysis and evaluation will inevitably need to take place *before* the actual classroom events and will involve the teacher in anticipating and planning for such issues as curriculum coverage, resource needs and time factors. Other aspects can only occur in the classroom and will relate to ongoing features such as monitoring opportunities for children's contributions or interactions and physical considerations.

## *The teacher: Planning*

> You are a manager and monitor of teaching and learning. You would not expect managers in any other job to start a day's work without a plan which covered not only what will happen that day but months . . . ahead. You would expect a manager . . . to know the strongest and weakest part of his or her operation (Clemson and Clemson, 1991: 94).

A useful starting point for teachers is to examine next week's timetabled plans and analyse the balance represented in relation to a number of features (it will be assumed that similar general considerations have already been given to the year and termly plans). What opportunity and time is incorporated into next week for:

- particular curriculum subjects – this can be worked out in rough proportions even within a topic focus (Moyles, 1988b);
- different forms of teaching, e.g. whole class, group, individual, peer tutoring;
- opportunities to include different teaching and learning approaches;
- the teacher's preparation for each day and for up dating or revising planning;
- listening to individual children or group reading;
- the servicing of materials, e.g. replenishing paper or pencil supplies;
- the inclusion of, and discussions with, classroom assistants;
- following up any specific learning or class interest from the previous week;
- class exchanges or shared sessions;

- gathering together necessary resources;
- observing and assessing children's learning;
- planned visits, visitors or special events in class/school.

As Medland and Vitale (1984: 3) advise, classroom management encompasses 'all activities undertaken by teachers to ensure that academic materials are presented under maximally efficient conditions for learning'. Plans must be revised if, for example, there is found to be an imbalance in the amount of class teaching, or the resources from the museum service have failed to arrive. (If the plans are initially written in pencil, amendment will be simpler and neater.) Daily plans can then be established, ensuring that the general balances are also considered for each individual day.

What *actually* happens each week should also be noted: it is a good idea to write down during the day if possible (or at least at the end of the day, as it is better not to rely too heavily on memory) what factors ensured success in meeting objectives and which require a rethink. Far from being a straitjacket, such detailed planning allows the teacher to know when spontaneity itself will be beneficial to children in supporting intended learning.

Daily plans also generate their own questions of teachers:

1 What are my intentions for today's teaching and learning sessions? Do I have a clear focus for the children and for myself?
2 Why have I set these? Are they the most appropriate for today's daily timetable structure, children's learning, curriculum needs and so on?
3 Does the day have a logical pattern, balance and cohesion?
4 What time have I got and what time do I need?
5 What materials are needed and are these readily available? Who will get the materials for each session – teacher, children, other adult?
6 How will I present what I want the children to do?
7 How will children be grouped? Is it sufficiently varied?
8 How are they likely to respond – class, group, individuals? How will concentration be encouraged? Is there a balance between seat-based and more active sessions?
9 Is what children will do motivating and interesting? Would I want to do it myself? Is the range of activites sufficiently varied?
10 How will I use my time – managing or teaching?

11 Are there any 'sticky' points in the day which should be anticipated, e.g. a changeover with another teacher?
12 Have I thought about minimizing any potential behaviour problems?
13 What about those children who finish early?
14 Will children know where to put completed work?
15 Will children know what to do if they have a query?
16 What about those who will not finish in the given time?
17 How will the children and I assess the outcomes of learning and gain and give feedback?
18 Will I be able to build on that learning during the week?

Some other factors in relation to the classroom teaching which are likely to require investigation include:

1 Approaches to individual children, e.g. are they all treated equally; do they receive similar amounts of time over a week; do they all have opportunity to work with other children; use different areas of the classroom; work on different aspects of the curriculum; are they treated similarly irrespective of sex, race, age, personality, capability?
2 Examining the kind of model presented by the teacher in the classroom, e.g. if children are negative with each other is this in any way a reflection on the teacher's approach; if children do not value particular activities, is this a reflection of the attitude to that activity modelled consciously or unconsciously by the teacher; does the teacher 'avoid generalised assumptions about particular groups or children being especially wary of those relating to race, gender or social background' (Alexander *et al.*, 1992: 39)?
3 Curriculum areas which receive the focus of teacher attention, e.g. does the teacher spend all her day with the writing and maths tasks and mostly ignore art and design activities, role play situations or practical science?
4 Different periods of the day – are some sessions better than others for certain kinds of teaching, e.g. is concentration on a difficult task more likely to occur when the children come back from a windy playtime, a very hot playtime, cold play-time, indoor playtime, after a long assembly?
5 Teacher's contact with individuals, e.g. how often is the teacher able to make contact with individual children each day or week; is this positive or negative contact; does it cover different curriculum areas; do all children have the opportunity to work

alongside the teacher in a concentrated group session; does the teacher monitor any differences in approach to certain individuals and is this justifiable?

6  Use made of records, e.g. is children's work planned through ongoing monitoring of progress and achievements; is the analysis of one session's teaching used to inform the planning for the next; are National Curriculum programmes of study a clear part of plans for teaching and learning; is progression adequately planned for all children within each subject?

7  Structure of the day, e.g. are there times when things appear to run very smoothly or not so smoothly; are activity change-over times anticipated or does everyone make a rush when the bell goes; is good use made of small periods of time prior to a changeover?

8  Does the teacher react to what is seen and heard rather than to what is interpreted; what steps can be taken to remove biases; do teachers notice the expected and the unanticipated?

9  Are high standards always expected and strived for, and are they within the reach of teachers and children?

10  How are intentions and instructions given and received?

---

*Example of the latter*

The teacher with a class of year 4 children spent some time in explaining exactly what the three different groups of children would be doing during the first session of the day, how they should set about it and the learning intentions. However, as the children went off to their tasks, there was much confusion and argument as to the tasks. The teacher noted this, talked to the children and realized that three different batches of instructions without opportunity for question or reiteration had created the problem. The teacher felt, however, that whole class instructions were still the best way of using available time, but an opportunity for the children to respond was the missing ingredient. The next session's explanation was done in the same way, but before each group was despatched to their tasks, the teacher spent a few moments asking them to outline to him the sequence of their activity. Each group was then able to approach their task with confidence.

*The physical learning environment: Space, movement and resources*

In addition to those aspects highlighted in Chapter 2, a few further aspects that are likely to require investigation include:

1  *Use of space*: how is each area used and for what proportion of the day; is the carpet area regularly occupied or used only at the beginning and end of the day; is there space for the teacher to walk round and monitor activities and teach groups and individuals; is the sink area bombarded by children at certain times of the day; what percentage of the classroom is in regular use each day?

2  *Furniture*: is there too much, too little; does it have all necessary rubber stoppers or feet or is there constant scraping of chair/table legs which deters concentration; are cupboards, shelves and surfaces constantly messy and, if so, is sufficient attention and time given to adequate tidying away; is all the furniture used and, therefore, necessary; are there chairs readily available for classroom helpers; is the furniture appropriately arranged to allow necessary groupings or flexibility of grouping; does the location of children's personal storage facility create human traffic jams?

3  *Movement patterns*: which areas constantly seem to be crowded or empty; if children are expected to line up at the door, does furniture inhibit this occurring in a civilized manner; is jostling noticed in and around particular areas of the room and what is the reason; can visitors enter and leave without climbing over children and furniture?

4  *Light/air*: are children constantly screwing up their eyes or looking sleepy; do at least some of the windows open effectively and is the necessary opening gadget readily to hand (but safely stored); do fluorescent lights flicker aggravatingly; are lights kept on unnecessarily or, alternatively, not used when needed; are some areas of the room darker than others and should something be done about this, either relocating a working bay or requesting provision of better lighting?

5  *Safety features*: do children suffer splinters from the furniture; are any chairs rickety or have gaps where fingers can get trapped; are there any trailing cables, loose carpet edges or similar over which children (and adults) may trip; is electrical equipment safety-checked periodically; are craft knives stored where the teacher can monitor their collection and use; does the use of water or sand present a safety hazard and what can

be done about it; do children step on each other's fingers as they move to sit on the carpet and how can this be avoided; can children reach items in regular use without climbing on furniture?

6  *Materials and resources*: have they been inspected in relation to presentation of equal opportunities across the board; are there any oblique messages in resource provision, e.g. does the home corner only have middle-class, Western cultural equipment; can children readily locate and access what they regularly need; can the teacher readily check equipment in frequent use, e.g. pencils, rubbers, scissors; is the computer used fully whenever it is available; are tape-recorders and calculators available as needed, working satisfactorily and who is responsible for their maintenance and safe-keeping; can other adults who use the classroom locate and return equipment; are resources used innovatively and flexibly, e.g. are the same things set out in different ways to create necessary variety within limited resources and materials?

7  *Use of schools' broadcasts*: do you incorporate these into the school day/week; for what reasons; is the listening or viewing preceded by a teaching/learning session; is full use made of the broadcasts in feedback and follow-up with the children; are programmes carefully selected to fit in with current curriculum plans; is it necessary and appropriate for all children to be involved; what do such broadcasts provide to enrich children's curricular experiences?

8  *Classroom displays*: are three-dimensional display areas dumping grounds; do display boards reflect current work, have a fresh appearance and is the work used by the teacher and children; are plants and animals cared for appropriately and systematically; does the classroom look inviting, appealing, exciting and cared for?

9  *Leaving the class area*: what do children need to do in order to signal their intention to leave the classroom area for toileting or other purposes; is there a system for monitoring their return; is there/should there be a limit to the number of children who may leave the classroom at the same time; how are the children facilitated to use library or resource areas outside the classroom; are learning spaces outside the class area adequately used; does their use interefere with other classes; how are the children using these areas monitored; are children sent on errands and do they understand their responsibilities?

10  *Noise and acoustic*s: are the levels appropriate for teaching

and learning purposes; is the teacher aware of his or her own tolerances in relation to the working noise of the classroom?

---

*Example of the latter*

A teacher of year 2 children was concerned that they seemed not to be making progress with phonic teaching despite her working very hard with groups to cover the consonant blends 'ch', 'sh', 'th', 'wh', 'ph': after two or three sessions few children were able to use the blends effectively. When the teacher analysed the situation by taping the next teaching session, she realized that because of the working noise from the nearby science area, it was unlikely that the children could differentiate clearly between the sounds. The work was then done with the whole class in a quieter session and the children began to make progress.

---

*Constraints external to the individual class base*

Some factors that require monitoring will be ones external to your classroom or, more specifically, aspects of the learning environment which are whole school issues; for example, noise from other class bases, frequent interruptions at crucial points, windows which will not open and result in a stuffy classroom where children appear sleepy. Use a brief amount of time one week gathering and writing a list of these points. Then cross out those things about which there is really *nothing* you can do to expedite change, e.g. the busy road on your doorstep which means you have regular and insistent traffic noise. Review the remaining factors and prioritize in relation to the level of hindrance or annoyance to you, then take one a week and deal with it (remember to incorporate it in weekly plans).

Where such factors involve others within the school, have a 'pet annoyance' session at a staff meeting. It is surprising how often several people have the same difficulties but have not verbalized them. A similar idea relates to unwanted or unused equipment in a class with the whole staff pooling unwanted items and offering them up to others. If no-one claims or needs the equipment, this constitutes a good resource weeding-out exercise – check on disposal of items with the head, however, before filing under bin!

*The children: What do they do and how do they do it?*

'Good teaching does not merely keep step with the pupils but challenges and stretches their thinking' (Alexander *et al.*, 1992: 36). In support of those aspects already discussed in Chapters 3 and 4, teachers need to consider the significance for learning opportunities within the classroom environment of:

- Current routines and whether they help or hinder children's learning.
- Each child's starting point and what can reasonably be expected in the way of activity outcomes, progress and attainment over each day, week and longer term. How can children be encouraged to work to targets and how can the teacher establish these with individuals?
- Task appropriateness – are opportunities provided for consolidation, practice, building on understanding and skills, developing new ideas and concepts, thinking creatively and imaginatively; and in what proportions are these opportunities available, e.g. are the children's activities mostly related to practice or are new learning opportunities available?
- Opportunities for choice and independence – do children have to refer to the teacher for every aspect of their activities; is there a balance between teacher-led tasks and children-led tasks and are the children aware of the differences; are genuine open-ended activities available to the children some of the time; are children shielded from learning through mistakes or are they taught to tolerate error as a learning process?
- Monitoring of individual children in order to learn about the experiences of the day from a child's perception.
- Quantity and quality of tasks children actually complete in a day.

---

*Example of the latter two*

Especially for the less experienced teacher, vital information should be gathered on what the children have actually been involved in during the day. By itself, this will give only limited quantitative information, but through marking and discussion with children, qualitative aspects will be revealed. Even very young children are capable of ticking their names off on a prepared class or group sheet when an activity has been completed and they can make their own qualitative statement by being encouraged to put one tick for 'I did it OK' or two ticks for 'I really enjoyed it'. Some teachers and children prefer drawing faces to show the attitude to the completed activity, with a smiley face, straight-mouth face or sad face indicating levels of enjoyment and satisfaction with the task. Similarly, children can write their names on a task sheet when they have finished or add their name card to a pocket marked 'History task' or 'Maths assignment'. Transferred to records, teachers will be able to monitor, against their current teaching plans, tasks completed with perhaps a qualitative statement through a coded system such as that shown in Figure 7.1.

Evidence will also be gained as to the quantity and quality of children's work, which should in itself generate questions about individuals and their capacity to undertake certain tasks. Why do some children work so much slower or quicker than others? Monitoring an individual child at either extreme for a day, perhaps noting every 5 minutes or so what they are doing at that time (or children doing the monitoring for themselves, which they find very exciting!), will give valuable information about how a child's time is utilized.

### Time availability and use

Considerable attention has already been given to the identification of time available in Chapter 5 and earlier in this chapter and curriculum time is clearly the most crucial of all aspects. Examples of a few other points warrant exploration.

1 *Time for observation and assessment processes*: how possible is it to observe for these purposes in the current classroom situation; if you sit down to work with a group what happens to the rest of the children; are they clear about *all* the available classroom 'resources', including other children, or is their first port of call always the teacher; are you clear about what you are observing for in the given time (use a checklist) or that you are observing generally for a stated period to see how children respond to a particular activity; have you explained in some way to the rest of the class what you are doing and why; can other children genuinely get on with the types of activities set (are they well-matched to children's present needs)?

*Figure 7.1* A matrix record showing a way of making simple qualitative statements regarding children's learning of concepts

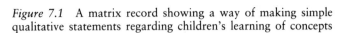

| | Maths - Shape 1 | Maths - Shape 2 | Maths - Measures 1 | Maths - Measures 2 | Maths - Measures 3 | Maths - Number 1 | Maths - Number 2 | Maths - Number 3 |
|---|---|---|---|---|---|---|---|---|
| Child A | ◮ | ∠ | ◮ | / | | ◮ | △ | |
| Child B | ◮ | ∠ | | / | | ◮ | △ | |
| Child C | ◮ | / | | / | | ◮ | / | |
| Child D | ◮ | / | ◮ | △ | / | ◮ | △ | / |

Key:

/ = Child just started on this concept

∠ = Child has had further experience of concept

△ = Child has done reinforcement activity(ies)

◮ = Child has this concept established at this time

2 *Interruptions*: how many interruptions do you have in a day/ week (make a note each time you are interrupted either by adults or children over a period of a week); is the reason for interruption justifiable or could it be avoided?

3 *Time quality*: is the time used by children in the day quality time? A simple, if rather subjective, activity for teachers to assess this is given in Figure 7.2.

4 *Time spent by the teacher, children, other adults*: are you fully aware of how children's time is spent or totally absorbed in your own time use; do classroom helpers spend long periods of

*Figure 7.2* Charting the quality (albeit subjectively) of children's use of time in the school day

| Child's name | Quality of experience | | | | | Quality of outcome | | | | | General comment |
|---|---|---|---|---|---|---|---|---|---|---|---|
| Child A | 1 | (2) | 3 | 4 | 5 | (1) | 2 | 3 | 4 | 5 | Uncertain. Never got into it -unwell!? |
| Child B | 1 | 2 | 3 | 4 | (5) | 1 | 2 | 3 | 4 | (5) | } Worked well together. |
| Child C | 1 | 2 | 3 | (4) | 5 | 1 | 2 | 3 | 4 | (5) | |
| Child D | 1 | 2 | 3 | 4 | (5) | 1 | 2 | (3) | 4 | 5 | Preferred exp. to task! |
| Child E | 1 | 2 | (3) | 4 | 5 | 1 | 2 | 3 | (4) | 5 | |
| Child F | 1 | 2 | (3) | 4 | 5 | 1 | 2 | (3) | 4 | 5 | |
| ......... | | | | | | | | | | | |
| ......... | | | | | | | | | | | |

1 = poor quality

5 = high quality

time doing little while you are explaining activities to children; have you estimated the shortest and longest time children will need to complete particular tasks; what about the children who complete earlier or later than the others; are children aware of how much time they have for a particular activity or can it just go on all day?

---

*Example of on aspect of this final point*

James and Gurpreet (both aged 9 years) always finish their work before the other children and are then allowed to choose a task. They normally select a construction set which then encourages Mohinda and Thomas, who rarely complete their tasks, to leave what they are doing and join the construction activity. What should the teacher do? Are the tasks given to James and Gurpreet too easy? Or are the tasks given to Mohinda and Thomas too difficult? As the latter pair rarely have the chance to use the constructional materials because of being slow to finish, could their task be based around that equipment? How could the teacher make better use of the children's time in relation to their interests? Could the children be encouraged to develop their own strategies for using time effectively? What monitoring and evaluation strategies could the teacher use to find out?

---

A simple sheet for monitoring the use of classroom time in a variety of circumstances is given in Figure 7.3. Many researchers actually operate such charts in minutes or less, though this would be less feasible for a class teacher or untrained observer because of the quantity of data it generates.

*Working with other adults*

The major questions in relation to monitoring, analysing and evaluating the involvement of others relate to:

1 *The quality of children's experiences with other adults*: are helpers confident in the handling of children and in the activities they undertake; are they aware of different strategies for gaining children's enthusiasm and concentration; is the time with children used to the fullest possible extent; is their work planned systematically and sequentially so that they see children's

*Figure 7.3* Basic chart for sampling the use of teacher time

| Activity | 5m | 5m | 5m | 5m | 5m | 5m | 5m | 5m | 5m | 5m | 5m | 5m | 5m |
|---|---|---|---|---|---|---|---|---|---|---|---|---|---|
| Talking to whole class | | | | | | | | | | | | | |
| Talking to individual children | | | | | | | | | | | | | |
| Talking to other adults | | | | | | | | | | | | | |
| Dealing with behaviour | | | | | | | | | | | | | |
| Doing the register | | | | | | | | | | | | | |
| Marking children's work | | | | | | | | | | | | | |
| Collecting money | | | | | | | | | | | | | |
| Organizing resources | | | | | | | | | | | | | |
| Cutting paper/mixing paints | | | | | | | | | | | | | |
| Tidying the classroom | | | | | | | | | | | | | |
| . . . . . . . . . . . | | | | | | | | | | | | | |
| . . . . . . . . . . . | | | | | | | | | | | | | |
| . . . . . . . . . . . | | | | | | | | | | | | | |
| . . . . . . . . . . . | | | | | | | | | | | | | |

The chart is kept in a handy place and every 5 minutes the teacher (or observer) marks which tasks were being undertaken at the time. Across the full hour covered by the chart, it is possible to get a general view of how the time was used. It is necessary to undertake this activity over different periods of the day and different days of the week in order to get a representative sample.

The chart can be adapted to any period of time from 10 seconds to 30 minutes.

It can be used for teacher time or adapted to examine children's use of time, the amount of time a particular area/bay is used or classroom helper's time.

progress; are helpers aware of how to give appropriate praise and encouragement to children?

2  *The quality of the teacher's experience in working with other adults*: does the teacher set up the situation to everyone's advantage and satisfaction; are all helpers clear about their role, time available, any peripheral events about which they need to know, e.g. going to assembly; is time available for helpers to discuss the activity with the teacher before and after the session; are helpers' own skills being used to the full; does the teacher learn more about individual children from having other adults involved; do helpers receive praise and encouragement from the teacher to sustain their interest and involvement?

3  *The use of a recording system for other adults*: do helpers understand what learning intentions they are attempting to meet; what information is required for children's learning to be evaluated; how do they monitor what children appear to be learning; have they been given, or developed for themselves, a checklist of skills and knowledge to look out for; are helpers asked to make objective notes on how well different children do on the task?

4  *Responsibility*: can other people such as the caretaker be encouraged – either by individual teachers or by the school staff as a whole – to be responsible for some of the classroom safety factors, e.g. furniture, cables; could a parent or ancillary helper be given the task of periodically checking resources for missing pieces, sharp edges, rusty blades?

5  *The value of visits and specific visitors*: did the children learn something lasting and worthwhile from this venture; how does the teacher know; could that learning have been achieved in any other way; how will the visit be followed up; how has the visit been recorded; do the children remember the major features several weeks later?

---

*Example of the latter*

Children in a year 6 class have been investigating birds of prey as part of a topic on food chains, and owls had become a particular favourite. After 3 weeks of working on the topic, the teacher invited into school a local person who had made a particular study of owls and who regularly retrieved baby owls in peril, reared them and then released them into the wild. On the day of the visit, one group of children worked with the teacher, exploring the kind of questions they would ask the visitor about owls by looking through some of the investigations they had already made and identifying incomplete aspects of their own knowledge. Another group completed a local scale map they had devised to try to identify likely owl habitats; they also planned questions they would ask the visitor about where owls were likely to be found, what tell-tale signs they could look for and so on. The third group, in the company of a parent helper, thought about what the visitor to the classroom might like to see about the work they had already done, and put together a display of children's activity outcomes, pictures, writing, graphs and so on. They also decided the visitor, including the owl, might like a drink and organized, with the parent's and kitchen staff's help, suitable refreshments. The teacher had made a tape-recorder and camera available and chose two pairs of children to record the event.

The visit was extremely successful, giving the children a great deal of information and first-hand experiences on which to build. Owls stayed very much a feature of this class's life for a very long time with assembly, movement activities, drama and other aspects reflecting an owl theme. Books were made which became part of the class library and were regularly discussed and learning revisited and reviewed. The work on habitats through map work motivated children to investigate other animal homes, which led neatly into a planned programme of the construction of homes in other countries. A quality experience all round.

## Final comments

It has been necessary in the space available to make many generalizations regarding the monitoring, analysing and evaluating of practice: not everything will necessarily apply to everyone. However, it is easy to dismiss many things which do apply in individual teacher's classrooms in the name of 'not being able to fit everything in' – understandable but not always justifiable, as should have become clear through some of the activities. Pollard and Tann (1987: 4) suggest that the hallmark of a reflective teacher is open-mindedness, whole-heartedness and responsibility. Monitoring, analysing and evaluating the classroom certainly requires these in good measure, for the processes cannot be successful without such commitment by the teacher.

The classroom management skills of any teacher are subject to a most widespread scrutiny: every one of us has been a school pupil at some time and, therefore, has implicit beliefs about what is a good classroom and class teacher (Braine *et al.*, 1990: 125). What is certain, is whether or not teachers themselves evaluate their own classroom practices, we can be sure that other people continually do so and are influenced by many of the factors explored in this chapter.

The challenges have now been made from central government and doubts cast as to the effectiveness of existing primary teaching, whether we believe these are justifiable or not. This renders it an opportune time to reflect on our practices, acquire knowledge of its best features and make considered changes to those aspects found wanting. In the name of accountability, we also need to be *seen* to be taking such action and to be articulating cogently and explicitly which classroom practices offer the best possible learning opportunities for children. It is appropriate to add that the highly satisfactory progress and attainment of all the children are a sure sign that the classroom organization and management is effective.

# 8

---

# Conclusion:
# The primary classroom –
# a place and a time

> The longest journey in the world is the journey from the head
> to the heart – and the shortest is from the heart to the head
> (attributed to Abdu'l-Baha earlier this century, source un-
> known).

As has consistently been shown throughout this book, being a
proactive teacher means accepting many challenges at a level of
reflection which the 'busyness' of primary teaching tends instinctively to deny. Primary teachers are not simply educators of, but
carers for, children, and therefore more often than not understandably find the heart ruling the head. Creating a situation of
balance between the two is, undoubtedly, the optimal way of
ensuring progress in teaching and learning. The challenges and
dilemmas of creating a quality learning environment through
classroom organization and management processes must be confronted by all teachers. Politically, the issue is poised to become a
critical feature of the 1990s, with both the extended classroom
training of new entrants to the profession and major discussion
being prompted by the government through reports such as that
presented by Alexander *et al.*, 1992.

At the end of the day, however, no-one can tell class teachers
how to organize their particular classrooms: the variables of
teachers, children, resources, physical space, expectations and school
ethos (the final portion of the diagram in Fig. I.1 in the Introduction), are too extensive. It would have been inappropriate for me

*Figure 8.1*   Some basic factors influencing teachers' classroom organization and management, both internal and external to the school

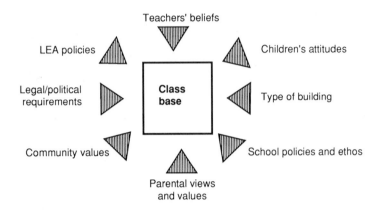

to give specific timetables or other exemplars for associated reasons. Elements of good practice can be identified, discussed, teachers' awareness heightened, questions raised, but only the individual teacher, in a particular classroom context, can translate the results into effective practice through synthesizing these into a coherent plan for his or her own context. Teachers can find themselves isolated in mobile classrooms a significant distance from the main school or working alongside several other teachers in a huge open-plan area. Whatever the circumstance, the specific features dealt with in this book – philosophies of teaching, developing the learning environment, the children, resources and materials, time factors, working with other adults and decisions arising from continual evaluation of classroom processes – have to be addressed by every teacher.

Schools were built at different periods in history and each reflects the philosophy of the time and each struggles to accommodate current ideologies and presents untold constraints but, as has been said many times, anything works for those who are convinced it will. As Cooper (1985: 267) reports, however, many teachers do operate against all odds. Many factors influence teachers' classroom organization and management, both internal and external to the school, as can be seen in Figure 8.1.

Ultimately, professionalism is about making your own decisions and actions based on carefully conceived personal constructs with a sound basis – that is what separates out the 'professional'. Such professionals are striving hard for classroom success at all levels. A majority of children can read and a majority of class teachers do their job effectively and could do even better given more supporting circumstances being developed inside schools and opportunities for reflection through in-service education beyond the school. Time to work alongside other colleagues in their classrooms and open up the somewhat dated one-teacher-one-class system must be faced.

Despite a wealth of research into effective teaching, both in Britain and the USA, very little research has been done on what constitutes an effective classroom environment. Hopefully, the current moves towards the identification of competencies in teaching will lead to a growing amount of research into classrooms which will more directly link pedagogical and practical considerations and give ammunition for providing teachers and children with the best possible learning environment.

A few studies have given credence to serious thinking regarding the physical context in which education takes place. In the USA, for example, Evertson (1989) undertook research in an attempt to improve elementary teachers' classroom management at the start of a school year through the provision of a pre-term in-service course on the main issues. She found that

> treatment group teachers exceeded the control group in use of key management principles taught in the workshops, had better student task engagement, and had less inappropriate behaviour.

The course covered a majority of the issues already discussed in this book and appeared to raise participants' awareness of those things which they confronted daily within the classroom which, to be effective, command planning and forethought.

In Britain, the Elton Report (DES, 1989: 88) emphasized the importance to school discipline of the quality of the environment and cared-for buildings, in which damage is promptly repaired and children's work attractively displayed. The committee also concluded that teachers need to be helped to become better classroom managers in order to reduce unwanted behaviours among children (p. 12). Other researchers have focused upon children's responses to the learning environment. Coulby and Coulby (1990), for example, pointed out that children are more likely to respect their classroom if they are involved in decisions about its layout.

The overriding research has, however, been into effective teaching (some studies were discussed in Chapter 1), a significant part of which relates to organizational issues. Mortimore *et al.* (1988)

*Classroom organization has been an implicit element in classroom interactions for a very long time.*

identified 12 key factors of teaching effectiveness in their study, of which seven have a direct relationship with classroom management issues, namely: well-structured sessions and days, intellectually challenging teaching in a variety of styles and methods, a work-centred environment, limited foci within sessions, maximum communication between teachers and pupils, record keeping and a positive climate. Lemlech (1979: 262) identified teachers' methodological skills as one of three major components upon which teacher competence could be assessed.

Student teachers show evidence daily of how much stress can be saved by being suitably organized for the teaching day ahead and having a range of management strategies at one's fingertips. Energy used in having constantly to react to management crises means less energy available for teaching. Energy used in securing a structured and workable learning environment gives confidence and security in handling teaching and learning processes.

Classroom organization has been an implicit element in classroom interactions for a very long time – indeed, a key element. It has now been given the direct attention it deserves and requires, which should enable primary teachers to achieve even more effective practice. However, effective practice will, no doubt, mean change for some teachers and the intentions of this book were first, to allow readers to identify their strengths and build on them and, secondly, to identify where specific changes could encourage them to become more effective and develop further success strategies. It would be unwise to change everything at once; start slowly, but DO START – the ultimate benefits for teacher and children will be many if intentions for change are clear and systematic.

The final activity is intended to set teachers thinking about their own class bases and the motives behind their creation and management of children's learning within it. Those questions which generate the most hesitation are likely to be the ones worth addressing as the starting point for classroom reappraisal.

---

ACTIVITY 12

- What is your present class base like?
- How satisfied are you with it?
- Does it need any changes? Why/why not?
- How much time, on average, do you spend getting the classroom ready at the start of a term or half-term to receive children?
- When making plans for the classroom, what do you think of first – the curriculum, the children, other members of staff, the school policies . . .?
- What do you consider most important when making classroom organization plans – space, furniture, movement, light quality, noise, storage, resources and materials, display, safety, curriculum, your own beliefs, equal opportunities, behavioural expectations . . .?
- How do you organize resources – by subject, size, type, frequency of use, defined area in classroom, children's interest . . .?
- Which resources and materials do you organize first – books, maths equipment, science equipment, toys and games, writing materials, art materials, found materials . . .?
- What is your labelling system like?
- How do you mostly plan for grouping the children – by ability, friendship, sex, age group, random, common interest, task set . . .?
- Do you do anything to cater specifically for different gender needs, ethnic needs, individual/special needs?
- Do you organize any aspects with observation and assessment particularly in mind?
- Which of the following cause you most concern – time, space, resources, materials, assessment arrangements, types of grouping, whole class teaching, planning, keeping records, behaviour

problems, preparation requirements, safety, implementing the curriculum . . .?
- What will the classroom look and feel like to others who enter?
- Will the children understand and empathize with the classroom organization?

---

It is worthwhile remembering Shipman's words (1985: 2): 'In a classroom you won't win all the time!'

### Final thoughts

Doing justice to such a huge area is extremely difficult: it is so dependent, as has been repeatedly emphasized, on the beliefs and concerns of those involved and the physical conditions of the school and class base which are the starting point. I have occasionally had to remind myself to retain the focus on classroom organization and management – no easy feat because of what that encompasses, – a whole sociological system with educational intentions. While the whole book is essentially a very personal view, I have tried to give a selection of tried and tested strategies which are eminently flexible and adaptable to different teaching styles and person-alities. Discussion points to heighten awareness and encourage personalization of the issues have been posed throughout and selective references have been cited wherever these were thought to add to the general discussion.

There will still be many issues which have not been addressed or only briefly covered and about which teachers will want to know more. This can only be a good feature. If this book encourages and motivates teachers to reflect on the intentions and rationales which inform their decisions on primary classroom organization and management, then it, at least, will go some way towards meet-ing its objectives.

# References

Ahlberg, A. (1984). *Please Mrs. Butler.* Harmondsworth: Penguin.

Alexander, R. (1984). *Primary Teaching.* London: Holt, Rinehart and Winston.

Alexander, R., Willcocks, J. and Kinder, K. (1989). *Changing Primary Practice.* Lewes: Falmer Press.

Alexander, R., Rose, J. and Woodhead, C. (1992). *Curriculum Organisation and Classroom Practice in Primary Schools: A Discussion Paper.* London: DES.

Anderson, L. and Burns, R. (1989). *Research in Classrooms: The Study of Teachers and Instruction.* Oxford: Pergamon Press.

Arnold, R. (1988). Making the best use of teacher time. In Craig, I. (ed.) *Managing the Primary Classroom.* Harlow: Longman.

Ashton, P. (1981). Primary teachers' aims. In Simon, B. and Willcocks, J. (eds) *Research and Practice in the Primary Classroom.* London: Routledge and Kegan Paul.

Ausubel, D.P., Novak, J.D. and Hanesian, H. (1978). *Educational Psychology: A Cognitive View*, 2nd edn. New York: Holt, Rinehart and Winston.

Ball, S., Hull, R., Skelton, M. and Tudor, R. (1984). The tyranny of the devil's mill: Time on task at school. In Delamont, S. (ed.) *Readings on Interaction in the Classroom: Contemporary Sociology of the School.* London: Methuen.

Bennett, N. and Cass, A. (1988). The effects of group composition on group interactive processes and pupil understanding. *British Educational Research Journal*, 15(1), 19–32.

Bennett, N. and Kell, J. (1989). *A Good Start? Four Year Olds in Infant Schools.* Oxford: Blackwell.

Bennett, N., Desforges, C., Cockburn, A. and Wilkinson, B. (1984). *The*

*Quality of Pupil Learning Experiences.* London: Lawrence Erlbaum Associates.

Bentley, D. and Rowe, A. (1991). *Group Reading in the Primary School.* Reading: Language Information Centre, University of Reading.

Berlak, A.C. and Berlak, H. (1981). *Dilemmas of Schooling.* London: Methuen.

Biott, C. (1984). Getting on without the teacher: Primary school pupils in cooperative groups. *Collaborative Research Paper 1.* Sunderland: Centre for Educational Research and Development, Sunderland Polytechnic.

Blatchford, P. (1989). *Playtime in the Primary School.* Windsor: NFER/Nelson.

Braine, M., Kerry, D. and Pilling, M. (1990). *Practical Classroom Management: A Guide for Secondary School Teachers.* London: David Fulton.

Broadfoot, P., Osborn, M., Gilly, M. and Pailett, A. (1988). What professional responsibility means to teachers. National contexts and classroom constants. *British Journal of Sociology of Education*, 9(3), 265–87.

Brophy, J. (1985). Interactions of male and female students with male and female teachers. In Wilkinson, L.G. and Marrett, G.B. (eds) *Gender Influence and Classroom Interaction.* Orlando: Academic Press.

Brown, S. and Cleave, S. (1991). *Four Year Olds in School: Quality Matters.* Slough: NFER.

Bruner, J. (1960). *The Process of Education.* New York: Random House.

Bruner, J. (1986). *Actual Minds: Possible Worlds.* Cambridge, Mass.: Harvard University Press.

Bruner, J. (1990). *Acts of Meaning.* Cambridge, Mass.: Harvard University Press.

Bull, S.L. and Solity, J.E. (1987). *Classroom Management: Principles to Practice.* London, Croom Helm.

Burns, R. (1982). *Self-concept, Development and Education.* London: Holt, Rinehart and Winston.

Calderhead, J. (1984). *Teachers' Classroom Decision-making.* London: Holt, Rinehart and Winston.

Campbell, A. and Brooker, N. (1990). Tom, Dick and/or Harriet: Some interventionist strategies against boys' sexist behaviour. In Tutchell, E. (ed.) *Dolls and Dungarees: Gender Issues in the Primary School Curriculum.* Milton Keynes: Open University Press.

Campbell, R.J. and Neill, S.R.St.J. (1990). *Thirteen Hundred and Thirty Days.* Warwick: AMMA/University of Warwick.

Campbell, R.J., Evans, L., Neill, S.R.St.J. and Packwood, A. (1991). *Workloads, Achievement and Stress.* Warwick: AMMA/University of Warwick.

Carr, W. and Kemmis, S. (1986). *Becoming Critical.* Lewes: Falmer Press.

Carroll, Lewis (1948). *The Hunting of the Snark.* London: Lighthouse Books/Chatto and Windus.

Casanova, U. (1989). Being the teacher helps students to learn. *Instructor*, May, pp. 12–13.

Chaikin, A., Sigler, E. and Derlega, V. (1975). Non-verbal mediators of teacher expectancy effects. *Journal of Personality and Social Psychology*, 30(1), 144–50.

Claxton, G. (1984). *Live and Learn: An Introduction to the Psychology of Growth and Change in Everyday Life*. London: Harper Row.

Claxton, G. (1989). *Being a Teacher: A Positive Approach to Change and Stress*. London: Cassell.

Claxton, G. (1990). *Teaching to Learn: A Direction for Education*. London: Cassell.

Claxton, G. (1991). *Educating the Inquiring Mind: The Challenge for School Science*. London: Cassell.

Clemson, D. and Clemson L. (1991). *The Really Practical Guide to Primary Assessment*. Cheltenham: Stanley Thornes.

Cooper, I. (1985). Teachers' assessments of primary school buildings: The role of the physical environment in education. *British Educational Research Journal*, 11, 253–69.

Cortazzi, M. (1991). *Primary Teaching – How it is: A Narrative Account*. London: David Fulton.

Coulby, J. and Coulby, D. (1990). Intervening in junior classrooms. In Docking, J. (ed.) *Alienation in the Junior School*. Lewes: Falmer Press.

Croll, P. (1986). *Systematic Classroom Observation*. Lewes: Falmer Press.

Crouse, P. and Davey, M. (1989). Collaborative learning: Insights from our children. *Language Arts*, 66(7), 756–66.

Cullingford, C. (1989). *The Primary Teacher: The Role of the Educator and the Purpose of Primary Education*. London, Cassell.

Cullingford, C. (1991). *The Inner World of the School: Children's Ideas about Schools*. London, Cassell.

Dadds, M. and Lofthouse, B. (1990). *The Study of Primary Education: A Source Book, Vol. 4: Classroom and Teaching Studies*, 2nd edn. Lewes: Falmer Press.

D'Arcy, S. (1990). Towards a non-sexist primary classroom. In Tutchell, E. (ed.) *Dolls and Dungarees: Gender Issues in the Primary School Curriculum*. Milton Keynes: Open University Press.

Davey, A. (1983). *Learning to be Prejudiced*. London: Arnold.

Day, C. (1990). *Insights into Teachers' Thinking and Practice*. Lewes, Falmer Press.

Day, C., Whitaker, P. and Wren, D. (1987). *Appraisal and Professional Development in the Primary School*. Milton Keynes: Open University Press.

Dennison, W. and Kirk, R. (1990). *Do, Review, Learn, Apply: A Simple Guide to Experiential Learning*. Oxford: Blackwell.

Denscombe, M. (1983). Ethnic group and friendship choice in the primary school. *Educational Research*, 25(3), 184–90.

Department of Education and Science (1989). *Discipline in Schools* (The Elton Report). London: HMSO.

Desforges, C. (ed.) (1989). *Early Childhood Education*. British Journal of Educational Psychology, Monograph Series 4. Edinburgh: Scottish Academic Press.

Design Council, The (1990). *Change in Practice*. London: The Design Council (booklet and video).

Docking, J. (1990). *Managing Behaviour in the Primary School*. London: David Fultin in association with Roehampton Institute.

Doherty, J. and Hier, B. (1988). Teacher expectations and specific judgements: A small-scale study of the effects of certain non-cognitive variables on teachers' academic predictions. *Educational Review*, 40(3), 333–48.

Downey, M.E. and Kelly, A.V. (1979). *Theory and Practice of Education*, 2nd edn. London: Harper Row.

Dunne, E. and Bennett, N. (1990). *Talking and Learning in Groups*. Basingstoke: Macmillan.

Eccles, J.S. and Blumenfeld, P. (1985). Classroom expectations and student grades: Are there differences and do they matter? In Wilkinson, L.G. and Marrett, G.B. (eds) *Gender Influence and Classroom Interaction*. Orlando: Academic Press.

Egan, K. (1988). *Primary Understanding*. New York: Routledge.

Ellsworth, J.A. and Monahan, A. (1989). Empower yourself for better classroom management. *Instructor*, August, pp. 72–5.

Entwhistle, N. (1988). *Styles of Learning and Teaching: An Integrated Outline of Educational Psychology for Students, Teachers and Lecturers*. London: David Fulton.

Everton, T. and Impey, G. (eds) (1990). *IT-INSET Partnership in Training: The Leciestershire Experience*. London: David Fulton.

Evertson, C.M. (1989). Improving elementary classroom management: A school-based training program for beginning the year. *Journal of Educational Research*, 83(2), 82–90.

Eysenck, H.J. (1990). Personality and school achievement. *Education Today*, 40(2), 3–16.

Farrell, C. (1989). More time to teach. *Learning*. July/August, pp. 52–4.

Field, T.M. (1980). Pre-school play: Effects of teacher/child ratios and organisation of the classroom space. *Child Study Journal*, 10(3), 191–205.

Fisher, R. (1990). *Teaching Children to Think*. Oxford: Blackwell.

Fitz-Gibbon, C. (1988). Peer tutoring as a teaching strategy. *Educational Management and Administration*, 16, 217–29.

French, J. (1986). Gender in the Classroom. *New Society*, 7, 405–6.

Galton, M. (1989). *Teaching in the Primary School*. London: David Fulton.

Galton, M. and Williamson, A. (1992). *Group Work in the Primary Classroom*. London: Routledge.

Galton, M., Simon, B. and Cross, P. (1980). *Inside the Primary Classroom*. London: Routledge and Kegan Paul.

Gardner, H. (1983). *Frames of Mind: The Theory of Multiple Intelligences*. London: Heinemann.

Gillespie, H. (1988). Using other adults in the classroom. In Craig, I. (ed.) *Managing the Primary Classroom*. Harlow: Longman.

Good, T.L. and Brophy, J.E. (1984). *Looking in Classrooms*, 3rd edn. New York: Harper Row.

Goodlad, J. (1983). A study of schooling: Some implications for school improvement. *Phi Delta Kappa*, 64, 552–8.

Goodlad, S. (1979). *Learning by Teaching: An Introduction to Tutoring.* London: City Service Volunteers.

Greenfield, J. (1984). A theory of the teacher in the learning activities of everyday life. In Rogoff, B. and Lave, J. (eds) *Everyday Cognition: Its Development in Social Contexts.* Cambridge, Mass.: Harvard University Press.

Haigh, G. (1990). *Managing Classroom Problems in the Primary School.* London: Paul Chapman.

Haigh, G. (1991). Not so dusty. *Times Educational Supplement,* 1 November, p. 24.

Halford, G.S. (1980). Towards a redefinition of cognitive developmental stages. In Kirby, J.R. and Biggs, J.B. (eds) *Cognition, Development and Instruction.* London: Academic Press.

Hartley, D. (1987). The time of their lives: Bureaucracy in the nursery school. In Pollard, A. (ed.) *Children and Their Primary Schools.* Lewes: Falmer Press.

Harvey, D. and Slatin, G. (1976). The relationships between a child's SES and teacher expectations: A test of the middle class bias hypothesis. *Social Forces,* 54(1), 140–59.

Haynes, M.E. (1987). *Make Every Minute Count.* London: Kogan Page.

Holt, J. (1991). *Learning All the Time.* Ticknell, Derbyshire: Education Now.

Hughes, M. (1989). The child as a learner: The contrasting views of developmental psychology and early education. In Desforges, C. (ed.) *Early Childhood Education.* British Journal of Educational Psychology, Monograph Series 4. Edinburgh: Scottish Academic Press.

Hull, C., Ruddock, J., Sigworth, A. and Daymond, G. (1985). *A Room Full of Children Thinking: Accounts of Classroom Research by Teachers.* York: SCDC Publications/London: Longmans.

Hull, J. (1990). *Classroom Skills: A Teacher's Guide.* London: David Fulton.

Huston, A.C. and Carpenter, C.J. (1985). Gender differences in pre-school classrooms: The effects of sex-type in activity choice. In Wilkinson, L.G. and Marrett, G.B. (eds) *Gender Influence and Classroom Interaction.* Orlando: Academic Press.

Jenks, J.M. and Kelly, J.M. (1986). *Don't Do ... Delegate: The Secret Power of Successful Managers.* London: Kogan Page.

Johnson, D. and Johnson, R. (1975). *Learning Together and Alone: Co-operation, Competition and Individualization.* Englewood Cliffs, N.J.: Prentice-Hall.

Jones, V.F. and Jones, L.S. (1986). *Comprehensive Classroom Management: Creating Positive Learning Environments,* 2nd edn. Boston, Mass.: Allyn and Bacon.

Karrby G. (1989). Children's conceptions of their own play. *International Journal of Early Childhood,* 21(2), 49–54.

King, R. (1978). *All Things Bright and Beautiful?* Chichester: John Wiley.

Knight, B. (1989). *Managing School Time.* Harlow: Longmans.

Kyriacou, C. (1991). *Essential Teaching Skills.* Oxford: Blackwell.

Leicestershire County Council (1989). *Keystages: Support Materials for Curriculum Planning and Assessment.* Leicester: LCC.

Lemlech, J.K. (1979). *Classroom Management*. New York: Harper Row.

Lockheed, M.E. (1985). Some determinants and consequences of sex segregation in the classroom. In Wilkinson, L.G. and Marrett, G.B. (eds) *Gender Influence and Classroom Interaction*. Orlando: Academic Press.

McAuley, H.J. (1990). Learning structures for the young child: A review of the literature. *Early Child Development and Care*, 59, 87–124.

McLean, S.V. (1991). *The Human Encounter: Teachers and Children Living Together in Pre-school*. Lewes: Falmer Press.

Mahlios, M. (1989). The influence of cognitive style on the teaching practices of elementary teachers. *Early Child Development and Care*, 51, 89–107.

Makins, V. (1969). Child's eye view of teacher. *Times Educational Supplement*. 19 and 26 September.

Masheder, M. (1986). *Let's Cooperate*. London: Peace Education Project.

Medland, M. and Vitale, M. (1984). *Management of Classrooms*. New York: Holt, Rinehart and Winston.

Meighan, R. (1981). *A Sociology of Educating*. London: Holt, Rinehart and Winston.

Merrett, F. and Wheldall, K. (1990). *Positive Teaching in the Primary School*. London: Paul Chapman.

Moir, A. and Jessel, D. (1989). *Brain Sex*. London: Mandarin Books.

Morrison, K. and Ridley, K. (1988). *Curriculum Planning and the Primary School*. London: Paul Chapman.

Mortimore, P., Sammons, P., Stoll, L.D. and Ecob, R. (1988). *School Matters: The Junior Years*. Wells: Open Books.

Moyles, J.R. (1988a). *Self-evaluation: A Primary Teacher's Guide*. Windsor: NFER/Nelson.

Moyles, J.R. (1988b). Does the National Curriculum mean the end of child-centred learning? *Child Education*, 65, 11.

Moyles, J.R. (1989). *Just Playing? The Role and Status of Play in Early Childhood Education*. Milton Keynes: Open University Press.

Moyles, J.R. (1991). *Play as a Learning Process in Your Classroom*. London: Mary Glasgow.

Moyles, J.R. (1992). Just a matter of routine . . .? Organising for learning in the early years classroom. *Education 3–13*, 20(2).

Mumford, A. (1982). Learning styles and learning skills. *Journal of Management Development*, 1(2), 55–65.

Myers, S.S. (1990). The management of curriculum time as it relates to student engaged time. *Educational Review*, 42(1), 13–23.

Nash, B.C. (1981). The effects of classroom spatial organisation on four and five year old children learning. *British Journal of Educational Psychology*, 51, 44–55.

Nash, R. (1973). *Classrooms observed*. London: Routledge and Kegan Paul.

Neill, S.R. St.J. (1991). *Classroom Non-verbal Communication*. London: Routledge.

Nias, J. (1989). *Primary Teachers Talking: A Study of Teaching as Work*. London: Routledge.

Nisbet, J.D. and Shucksmith, J. (1986). *Learning Strategies.* London: Routledge and Kegan Paul.

Open University (1980). *Curriculum in Action: An Approach to Evaluation.* Milton Keynes: The Open University Press/Schools Council.

Palardy, M.J. (1969). 'What teachers believe: What children achieve.' *Elementary School Journal*, 69, 370–4.

Patel, P. (1991). Jokes are no laughing matter, says college chief. *Daily Telegraph*, 14 October, p. 3. Report of a series of lectures given by Dr Keith Cameron, Dean of the Faculty of Arts, Exeter University.

Pernet, R. (1989). *Effective Use of Time.* London: Education for Industrial Society.

Plowden Report, The (1967). *Children and Their Primary Schools.* Report of the Central Advisory Council for Education in England, 2 Vols. London: HMSO.

Pollard, A. (1985). *The Social World of the Primary School.* London: Holt, Rinehart and Winston.

Pollard, A. (1987). *Children and Their Primary Schools: A New Perspective.* Lewes: Falmer Press.

Pollard, A. and Tann, S. (1987). *Reflective Teaching in the Primary School: A Handbook for the Classroom.* London: Cassell.

Powell, M. and Solity, J. (1990). *Teachers in Control: Cracking the Code.* London: Routledge.

Pramling, I. (1988). Developing children's thinking about their own learning. *British Journal of Educational Psychology*, 58(3), 266–78.

Purchon, V. (1991). Room for improvement. *Times Educational Supplement*, 13 December, p. 22.

Raven, J. (1989). Parents, education and schooling. In Desforges, C. (ed.), *Early Childhood Education.* British Journal of Educational Psychology, Monograph Series 4. Edinburgh: Scottish Academic Press.

Richardson, N. (1984). *The Effective Use of Time.* London: Education for Industrial Society.

Riseborough, G.F. (1985). Pupils, teachers, careers and schooling: An empirical study. In Ball, S.J. and Goodson, L.F. (eds) *Teachers' Lives and Careers.* Lewes: Falmer Press.

Rodger, I.A. and Richardson, J.A.S. (1985). *Self-evaluation for Primary Schools.* London: Hodder and Stoughton.

Rogers, C. (1983). *Freedom to Learn for the 80s.* Columbus, Ohio: Charles E. Merrill.

Rose, S. (1983). Promoting social competence in children: A classroom approach to social and cognitive skill training. In LeCroy, C.W. (ed.) *Social Skills Training for Children and Youth.* New York: Haworth Press.

Rowlands, S. (1987). Child in control: towards an interpretive model of teaching and learning. In Pollard, A. *Children and their Primary Schools.* Lewes: Falmer Press.

Schools Examination and Assessment Council (*c*. 1990). *A Guide to Teacher Assessment (Pack C): A Source Book of Teacher Assessment.* London: Heinemann Educational.

Schools Council (1983). *Primary Practice: A Sequel to the Practical Curriculum.* Working Paper No. 75. London: Methuen Educational.

Sharan, S. (1980). Cooperative learning in small groups: Recent methods and effects on achievement, attitudes and ethnic relations. *Review of Educational Research,* 50, 241–71.

Shipman, M. (1985). *The Management of Learning in the Classroom.* London: Hodder and Stoughton.

Silveira, W.R. and Trafford, G. (1988). *Children Need Groups.* Aberdeen: Aberdeen University Press.

Simon, B. (1981). Towards a revitalized pedagogy. In Dadds, M. and Lofthouse, B. (eds) *The Study of Primary Education: A Source Book, Vol. 4: Classroom and Teaching Studies.* Lewes: Falmer Press.

Slavin, R. (1983). *Cooperative Learning.* New York: Longman.

Smith, L.A.H. (1985). *To Understand and to Help: The Life and Works of Susan Isaacs.* USA Associated University Presses Inc.

Smyth, J. (1990). A critical pedagogy of classroom practice. *Journal of Curriculum Studies,* 21(6), 483–502.

Solomon, D. and Kendall, A.J. (1979). *Children in Classrooms: An Investigation of Person–environment Interaction.* New York: Praeger.

Stones, E. (1979). *Psychopedagogy: Psychological Theory and Practice of Teaching.* London: Methuen.

Thody, A. (1990). Time to think. *Child Education,* 67(3), 14–15.

Thomas, N. (1985). *Improving Primary Schools.* London: ILEA.

Thomas, S. (1991). Upsetting the natural order. *Times Educational Supplement,* 4 October, p. 27.

Thompson, L. and Thompson, A. (eds) (1984). *What Learning Looks Like.* Schools Council Publications, Programme 2. York: Longmans for Schools Council.

Tizard, B. and Hughes, M. (1984). *Young Children Learning.* Glasgow: Fontana.

Tizard, B., Blatchford, P., Burke, J., Farquhar, C. and Plewis, I. (1988). *Young Children at School in the Inner City.* Hove: Lawrence Erlbaum Associates.

Topping, K. (1987). Peer tutored paired reading: outcome data from ten projects. *Educational Psychology,* 7(2), 133–45.

Topping, K. (1988). *The Peer Tutoring Handbook: Promote Cooperative Learning.* Beckenham: Croom Helm.

Trotter, A. and Wragg, E.C. (1990). A study of supply teachers. *Research Papers in Education,* 5(3), 251–76.

Turner, J. (1984). *Cognitive Development and Education.* London: Methuen.

Varley, H.M. and Busher, H. (1989). Just a minute . . .? – Managing interruptions in the junior school classroom. *Educational Studies,* 15(1), 53–65.

Vygotsky, L. (1978). *Mind in Society: The Development of Higher Psychological Processes.* Cambridge, Mass.: Harvard University Press.

Weinstein, C.S. and Woolfolk, A.E. (1981). The classroom setting as a source of expectation about teachers and pupils. *Journal of Experimental Psychology,* 1, 117–29.

Wells, G. (1987). *The Meaning Makers: Children Learning Language and Using Language to Learn.* Sevenoaks: Hodder and Stoughton.

Wenham, M. (1991). Education as interaction. *Journal of Philosophy of Education,* 25(2), 235–46.

West, C. and Wheldall, K. (1989). Waiting for teacher: The frequency and duration of times children spend waiting for teacher attention in infant school classrooms. *British Journal of Educational Research,* 15(2), 250–6.

Westmacott, E. and Cameron, R. (1988). *Behaviour can Change.* Basingstoke.

Wheldall, K. and Glynn, T. (1989). *Effective Classroom Learning.* Oxford: Blackwell.

Wheldall, K. and Olds, D. (1987). Of sex and seating: the effects of mixes and same-sex teaching arrangements in junior classroom. *New Zealand Journal of Educational Studies,* 22, 71–85.

Whitfield, A. (1991). Bill of rights with reality in-built. *Times Educational Supplement,* 13 December, p. 23.

Wilkinson, C. (1988). Arranging the classroom environment. In Craig, I. (ed.) *Managing the Primary Classroom.* Harlow: Longman.

Wittrock, M. (ed.) (1986). *Handbook of Research on Teaching.* New York: Macmillan.

Wolfendale, S. (in press). *All About Me.* Harlow: Longman.

Wood, D. (1986). Aspects of teaching and learning. In Richards, M. and Light, P. (eds). *Children of Social Worlds.* Cambridge: Polity Press.

Wood, D. (1988). *How Children Think and Learn.* Oxford: Basil Blackwell.

Wood, D. (1991). Aspects of teaching and learning. In Light, P., Sheldon, S. and Woodhead, M. (eds) *Learning to Think.* London: Routledge in association with The Open University.

Woods, P. (1990). *Teacher Skills and Strategies.* Lewes: Falmer Press.

Wragg, E. (1991). Thou shalt not covet thy neighbour's answers. *Times Educational Supplement,* 21 June, p. 15.

Wragg, E. and Wood, E. (1984). Pupils' appraisal of teaching. In Wragg, E. (ed.) *Classroom Teaching Skills: The Findings of the Teacher Education Project.* London: Croom Helm.

# Index